HISTORY OF THE SALEM WITCH HUNT (1692)

The Trials, The Accused, and The Legacy of Colonial Massachusetts

MICHAEL Jr. SCOTFIELD

Copyright © 2024 by Michael Jr. Scotfield

All rights reserved. No part of this book may be reproduced or transmitted in any form or by any means, electronic or mechanical, including photocopying, recording, or by any information storage and retrieval system, without permission in writing from the publisher.

The information provided in this book is designed to provide helpful information on the subjects discussed. The author and publisher disclaim any liability or loss in connection with the use or misuse of this information. It is recommended that readers consult with appropriate professionals before taking any actions based on the information in this book.

INTRODUCTION

In 1692, something terrible happened in Salem, a small town in Massachusetts. What started as a few girls acting strangely turned into a huge panic about witches. This event, known as the Salem witch trials, is one of the darkest times in early American history.

Salem was a tough place to live back then. The people worked hard and believed strongly in God. But they also had many problems with each other. Some families fought over land, while others just didn't get along. When accusations of witchcraft started, all these old problems made things worse.

The Salem witch hunt isn't just an old story about people believing in magic. It's about how fear can make people do awful things. It makes us ask important questions: How do we treat people fairly when we're scared? What happens when the people in charge abuse their power? How quickly can a community fall apart when people stop trusting each other?

In this book, we'll discover what life was like in Salem. We'll hear about the people who were accused of being witches and those who accused them. We'll learn about the judges who decided their fates and the brave few who spoke up against the trials.

We'll see how things like gender, money problems, and belief in the supernatural all played a part in this tragedy. We'll also look at how the Salem trials still matter today. Throughout history, there have been other times when people were unfairly accused and punished because of fear and paranoia.

As we read about Salem, we'll try to understand why it happened and what we can learn from it. The lessons from Salem are still important today. They remind us to be fair, to think clearly, and to be kind, especially when we're afraid.

So, let's begin our journey back to Salem in 1692. We'll see a world where people thought witches were real, where neighbors turned against each other, and where twenty innocent people lost their lives because of fear and confusion. The story of the Salem witch trials isn't just history – it's a warning about what can happen when fear takes over a community.

CHAPTER 1

The Spark in Salem Village

A Community on Edge

In 1692, Salem Village was a community simmering with tension, fear, and suspicion. This is a village that is located on the fringes of the Massachusetts Bay Colony, it was a place of hardship and unrest and it was like an insular farming village where nearly every aspect of life revolved around the church. The daily rhythm of existence was steeped in strict Puritan religious doctrine, which dictated not only personal behavior but also the fabric of the community. These were devout people, but their rigid moral code also created an environment where deviation from the norm could be seen as a sign of moral corruption—or worse, witchcraft.

Economically, Salem Village was a place of stark contrasts. Some families, particularly those in the eastern part of the village, were wealthier and more connected to the bustling port town of Salem Town, located just a few miles away. The wealthier villagers often engaged in commerce and trade, which created jealousy and resentment among the poorer farmers who relied solely on subsistence agriculture. The Putnam family, for example, were prominent landowners in the village and fiercely protective of their influence, while families like the Porters leaned toward the mercantile interests of Salem Town. This division created a deep social rift between those who saw the town's growing commercialism as a threat to traditional Puritan values and those who viewed it as an opportunity for prosperity.

Religious tension also exacerbated the situation. Salem Village was officially a part of Salem Town but sought autonomy, particularly when it came to spiritual matters. The village had its own church, but its ministers often found themselves entangled in bitter disputes with parishioners. Samuel Parris, who became the minister in 1689, was a particularly polarizing figure. Many villagers resented him for his demands for higher pay and his uncompromising stance on religious doctrine. His sermons were fiery, emphasizing the constant threat of the Devil's influence and the need for vigilance against sin. Parris's zealotry fanned the flames of an already anxious community, where spiritual matters were not just abstract concerns but life-or-death struggles for the soul of the village.

Moreover, the village's governance was chaotic and divisive. Disputes over property lines and rights to farmland often erupted into full-blown legal battles. For instance, many villagers still harbored grudges over long-standing property disputes with their neighbors. In such a small community, these disputes were personal, and they eroded any sense of unity. The communal fabric was fraying, and people were quick to suspect each other of wrongdoing, whether that meant theft, deceit, or even supernatural interference.

Daily life in Salem Village was an exercise in endurance. The harsh New England winters meant that survival was never guaranteed, and illness could sweep through a household or the entire village without warning. The fear of the unknown loomed large in the minds of villagers. If a cow fell ill or a crop failed, the first question many asked was, "Why?" However, In a world where the line between the natural and the supernatural was blurred, it was easy to see these misfortunes as signs of malevolent forces at work. The Puritan worldview embraced the idea that God—and by extension, the Devil—was directly involved in the events of everyday life. When bad things happened, people searched for a scapegoat, and in 1692, the Devil's agents were believed to be among them.

The role of women in this society added another layer of tension. Women were expected to be pious, submissive, and obedient, and yet they were seen as more vulnerable to the Devil's influence. The gender hierarchy in Salem Village was strict, and women who deviated from their prescribed roles—whether by being outspoken, independent, or too successful—were often looked at with suspicion. For example, some of the women who would later be accused of witchcraft, like Bridget Bishop, were known for their assertive personalities and defiance of traditional gender norms. In a community already teetering on the edge, such behavior was seen not just as rebellious but as dangerous.

Another layer of anxiety stemmed from the constant threat of Native American attacks. Salem Village was part of a frontier society, and memories of King Philip's War (1675–1678) were still fresh. Many of the villagers had lost family members or knew someone who had died in these brutal skirmishes. Fear of the "savage" other was a common theme in Puritan sermons, and this fear bled into the social consciousness. In times of stress, it wasn't difficult for the villagers to imagine that the Devil, too, could be lurking in the shadows, ready to strike through his earthly agents.

This combination of social, economic, and religious tensions created a highly combustible environment in Salem Village. Fears about spiritual purity, economic competition, and personal grudges coalesced into a community constantly on edge. People mistrusted their neighbors, whispered about each other behind closed doors, and looked for signs of the Devil's influence in everyday life. In such an atmosphere, all it took was a spark to ignite a full-blown witch hunt.

The "spark" would come from an unlikely place: the home of Reverend Samuel Parris, where his daughter Betty and niece Abigail Williams began exhibiting strange, unexplainable behaviors. Their fits, contortions, and strange utterances were unlike anything the villagers had seen before. Given the existing anxieties within the community, it didn't take long for accusations of witchcraft to start flying. The fear and paranoia that had been brewing for years finally exploded, and the Salem Witch Trials were born out of this volatile mix of personal vendettas, spiritual terror, and economic rivalry.

As 1692 unfolded, the people of Salem Village found themselves swept up in a frenzy of accusations and trials that would leave an indelible mark on their community—and on history itself. What had begun as a small Puritan farming settlement had, within a few short months, become the epicenter of one of the most infamous witch hunts in history. In many ways, the trials were not just about witchcraft, but about the deeper anxieties that plagued this fragile, fractious community. The legacy of that fear and division would haunt Salem for generations.

The Afflicted Girls

In 1692, religious community of Salem Village, Massachusetts, experienced an unseen terror. It all began with two young girls—Betty Parris, aged nine, and her cousin, Abigail Williams, eleven—whose strange behaviors would soon ignite a firestorm of agitation, fear, and accusation that would consume the village.

Betty was the daughter of Reverend Samuel Parris, the village's new minister, and Abigail was his niece. Both girls lived under the same roof, in the modest parsonage at the center of village life. Reverend Parris, a strict and imposing figure, had been brought to Salem to guide the community back to its Puritan roots. He preached fire-

and-brimstone sermons that stressed the dangers of the Devil's influence, creating an atmosphere already fraught with anxiety over sin and spiritual corruption.

The first signs of trouble appeared in early January, when Betty and Abigail began behaving in ways that left their family and neighbors baffled—and terrified. The girls complained of sharp pains, convulsed violently, screamed at invisible tormentors, and contorted their bodies into unnatural positions. They spoke in strange languages, barked like dogs, and fell into fits where they claimed to be attacked by unseen hands. Reverend Parris and his wife, desperate to understand what was happening, called in a local doctor, William Griggs. Unable to find a physical cause for the afflictions, Griggs suggested a chilling explanation: the girls were bewitched.

This diagnosis of witchcraft was hardly new in the Puritan world. Colonial Massachusetts was steeped in a belief system that saw the Devil and his minions as real, constant threats to the godly community. The idea that witches, as agents of the Devil, could cause physical harm or possess individuals to carry out evil deeds fit neatly within the Puritan worldview. Reverend Parris, already sensitive to any signs of spiritual danger in his congregation, was quick to embrace the notion that Satan had found his way into Salem.

But what could have caused such strange behaviors in Betty and Abigail? From a contemporary perspective, witchcraft seemed like the only plausible explanation. The afflicted girls' symptoms were consistent with popular beliefs about the effects of a witch's curse—bodily torments, strange visions, and fits. Moreover, the fact that both girls were closely tied to the village's religious authority figure likely lent weight to the diagnosis. If the minister's own family could be attacked, surely the whole community was in danger.

However, modern scholars have suggested a number of alternative explanations for the girls' behavior. One possibility is that they were suffering from a type of psychological stress. The strict and oppressive religious environment, combined with the social pressures on young girls, may have triggered what we now recognize as conversion disorder—a condition in which psychological stress manifests as physical symptoms. Others have speculated that the girls might have been unwittingly influenced by a desire for attention or power. In a society where children were expected to be seen and not heard, suddenly becoming the center of a village-wide crisis could have been intoxicating.

Another theory points to the possibility of environmental factors. Some historians have proposed that the girls could have been victims of ergot poisoning. Ergot is a fungus that can grow on rye and other grains, producing a substance that can cause hallucinations, convulsions, and other symptoms similar to what the girls experienced. The cold, damp winter conditions in Salem that year were ideal for the growth of ergot, and if contaminated grain had been consumed, it might explain the strange and erratic behaviors of the afflicted.

Betty and Abigail's backgrounds offer important clues as well. Both girls came from relatively privileged positions in Salem society. As the daughter and niece of the village minister, they were part of a household that wielded considerable influence. In a community where status was closely tied to one's relationship with the church, Betty and Abigail's afflictions were taken seriously from the outset. Their suffering carried more weight than it might have if they had been the children of a less prominent family.

The girls were also young, impressionable, and likely shaped by the religious and social environment around them. They would have been well-versed in the Puritan fear of the Devil and the ever-present possibility of his influence. It's not hard to observe that they might have internalized the fears and anxieties of the adults around them, especially given the sermons they likely heard from Reverend Parris, who often preached about the dangers of witchcraft and Satanic influence. In such a charged atmosphere, their fits and accusations could have been a reflection of the world they knew.

Regardless of the underlying causes, Betty and Abigail's behavior set off a chain reaction in Salem. Their afflictions were soon mirrored by other girls in the village, including Ann Putnam Jr., Elizabeth Hubbard, and Mary Walcott. The group of afflicted girls grew larger, their symptoms more dramatic, and their accusations more specific. They began to name names—initially accusing lower-status women like Tituba, the Parris family's enslaved servant, and Sarah Good, a homeless beggar.

As the accusations spread, the girls' role in the community shifted dramatically. From being relatively invisible members of Salem society, they became central figures in the unfolding drama. Their testimony would soon carry the weight of life and death, as the women they accused were arrested, tried, and in many cases executed. However, these young girls held the fate of the village in their hands, and their words would forever alter the course of Salem's history.

The actions of Betty Parris and Abigail Williams left a profound impact on the community. What started as isolated fits of rage soon spread through the village like wildfire, fueling suspicions, accusations, and fear. Their afflictions may have begun as an expression of personal turmoil or stress, but they tapped into deep-seated anxieties about sin, the Devil, and the fragility of the Puritan world. In a society where spiritual and social order were intertwined, the girls' behavior was more than a personal crisis—it became a communal catastrophe.

However, whether the girls were truly victims of witchcraft, suffering from psychological distress, or simply playing a role in a society that feared the Devil's presence, their actions set the stage for one of the darkest chapters in American history: the Salem witch trials.

Their story reveals the complex interplay between belief, fear, and power, and the far-reaching consequences that can arise when a community is driven by fear of the unknown.

Tituba's Fateful Confession

Tituba's fateful confession is one of the most pivotal moments in the Salem Witch Trials, where an already tense and suspicious environment quickly spiraled into fury.

A Stranger in a Foreign Land

Tituba was an enslaved woman, likely of Arawak or Carib descent, born in the West Indies. She was brought to Salem by Samuel Parris, the minister of the village, after he had returned from Barbados, where he had spent years managing his family's plantation. Life in the Parris household for Tituba would have been far from easy. As a slave, she was subject to the whims and demands of the family, and her foreignness marked her as "other" in the Puritan community. Not only did she physically stand out due to her likely darker skin, but her practices, mannerisms, and very being were considered foreign and suspicious by those who had little knowledge or understanding of her culture.

Within the Parris household, Tituba was tasked with caring for the family, including the minister's daughter, Betty, and his niece, Abigail Williams. The two girls, caught up in the strict and repressive atmosphere of Salem, began to experience strange fits and convulsions in early 1692. Their erratic behavior—screaming, contorting their bodies, and uttering nonsensical words—baffled the community. They were soon joined by other young girls in Salem, whose symptoms mirrored Betty's and Abigail's. The village began to panic, seeking explanations for these unnatural afflictions.

The Accusation and the Confession

Tituba, along with two other women, Sarah Good and Sarah Osborne, was one of the first to be accused of witchcraft. Unlike the other two, however, Tituba's lowly status as a slave made her a prime target for scapegoating. She was already a figure of suspicion due to her background. People whispered about the influence of her "heathen" origins, claiming she may have dabbled in dark practices learned from her homeland. When questioned, the village was not prepared for what would come next.

However , a scene played out where a small, cold room where Reverend Samuel Parris looms over her. His eyes narrow as he questions her, not only as her master but as a man who carries the moral weight of the village. The young girls who had been afflicted—Betty and Abigail—are watching from nearby, their faces contorted with fear and expectation. The air in the room is thick with tension. Parris presses her with relentless questions, demanding to know the source of the girls' afflictions.

In a soft, hesitant voice, Tituba begins to speak. At first, she denies the accusations, but under mounting pressure, something in her breaks. Whether out of desperation, fear of punishment, or a belief that her confession might save her life, Tituba starts weaving a tale that shocks everyone present. She claims she was visited by a tall man from Boston—presumably the Devil—who instructed her to sign his book. She describes strange creatures—a black dog, a yellow bird, and even a hog—that accompanied the man and threatened her if she refused his demands.

Her confession doesn't stop there. She implicates others, claiming that Sarah Good and Sarah Osborne, the other two accused women, were also part of this dark pact. The image of these women signing the Devil's book together and conspiring to torment the children of Salem electrifies the courtroom. In her words, the Devil's influence is no longer an abstract force but a real and immediate threat to the village. Her confession pours fuel on the already smoldering fears of witchcraft that had begun to consume Salem.

The Impact of Her Confession

Tituba's confession was far more than an admission of guilt; it was the spark that ignited a wildfire. By naming others as accomplices, she validated the growing difficulties that witches had infiltrated the community. The idea that there was an organized coven of witches operating in Salem, with the Devil at their helm, terrified the villagers. Her vivid descriptions of dark forces at work—the black dog, the strange birds—fueled the belief that there were supernatural entities at play, and this deeply religious community saw it as a battle between good and evil.

But why did Tituba confess in such a way? Some historians argue that her confession was strategic. As an enslaved woman, her status was already precarious. Confessing and weaving an elaborate tale may have been her way of saving herself from a harsher fate. In fact, while Sarah Good and Sarah Osborne were quickly convicted, Tituba's confession spared her immediate execution. She was imprisoned but survived the trials, suggesting that she may have understood the value of giving her accusers what they wanted: a narrative that confirmed their worst fears.

Yet, her position as an enslaved woman of non-European descent undoubtedly shaped how she was perceived. Puritan society, with its rigid social hierarchies and religious orthodoxy, saw Tituba as inherently suspicious. Her ethnicity and outsider status made her an easy target for accusations of witchcraft. There was already a prevailing belief among many European colonists that non-Christian, non-European people were more susceptible to the Devil's influence. Tituba's confession only confirmed their prejudices, reinforcing the notion that "heathen" peoples—whether from Africa, the Caribbean, or Native American tribes—were aligned with dark forces.

The Aftermath and Legacy

Tituba's confession did more than just condemn her; it set the tone for the subsequent trials. After her admission, the number of accusations skyrocketed. Dozens of men and women, young and old, were arrested and charged with witchcraft, often on the flimsiest of evidence—pointing fingers, spectral visions, and hearsay. Tituba's words had a ripple effect, not just in Salem but in the larger narrative of the trials.

Her confession also unviels the racial dynamics of the period. While many of the accused in the Salem Witch Trials were white, Tituba's confession thus reveals the ways in which race and servitude intersected with the fears of witchcraft. Her role as a woman of color who confessed to witchcraft, thereby confirming the worst suspicions of the white, Christian community, exemplifies how fears of the "other" could be weaponized during moments of social upheaval.

Eventually, Tituba survived the trials, though her fate after being imprisoned remains murky. Her confession, whether given out of fear or strategic self-preservation, left an indelible mark on the Salem Witch Trials and on the cultural memory of the event.

CHAPTER 2

The Kindling of Hysteria

From Accusations to Arrests

In the aftermath of Tituba's startling confession, a chain reaction of accusations began to sweep through the tight-knit communities of Salem and its surrounding villages.

As accusations began to fly, many of those targeted seemed to be individuals who were already on the outskirts of society—women like Sarah Good and Sarah Osborne, both of whom were easy to vilify due to their perceived nonconformity.

Once accusations were made, the path to arrest was swift and direct. If a person was suspected of witchcraft, they would be brought before local magistrates, who would determine whether there was enough evidence to proceed with formal charges. This evidence was often scant—based primarily on hearsay or spectral evidence, which was testimony that the spirit or specter of the accused had been seen committing acts of witchcraft. The highly subjective nature of spectral evidence, though controversial even at the time, was often accepted because of the overwhelming fear of the Devil's influence.

The process of turning suspicion into a formal arrest involved a blend of religious and legal procedures.

Magistrates such as Jonathan Corwin and John Hathorne played a key role in examining the accused, asking probing and often leading questions designed to elicit confessions or damning statements. The goal was not necessarily to determine innocence but to unearth further evidence of a broader conspiracy.

One of the most famous early accusers was Ann Putnam Jr., a twelve-year-old girl from a prominent family in Salem Village. Her father, Thomas Putnam, was a well-established figure in the community with a number of ongoing disputes, particularly over land. Ann's accusations were pivotal, as she implicated not just outcasts but also people from more respected families. Her claims carried weight, partly because of her father's influence, and they helped broaden the scope of the witch hunt, casting suspicion on individuals from different social strata. Her testimony would become one of the key threads that wove together the mounting panic.

The motivations behind the accusations were complex, and while religious fear was a driving force, underlying social dynamics also played a significant role in determining who would be accused. Women, particularly those who lived outside traditional gender roles or exhibited unusual behavior, were disproportionately targeted. This included women who were poor, widowed, or outspoken—categories that threatened the Puritan ideal of a submissive, godly woman. Men were not exempt, but they were often accused in connection with the women in their lives, such as husbands or sons of alleged witches.

In addition to social standing, economic competition often influenced who was accused. The colony was not immune to envy or greed, and in some cases, accusations of witchcraft were a convenient way to rid oneself of a rival. Property disputes, especially in a land-starved community like Salem, were sometimes settled through the court of witchcraft, as an accusation could lead to the accused losing their land and possessions. This created a perverse incentive for some to use the witch trials to further their own economic interests.

The speed at which accusations spread was alarming. The courtroom in Salem Village became a revolving door for the accused. Some, like Bridget Bishop, had faced accusations of witchcraft long before the 1692 hysteria began. Bishop, known for her independent spirit and tavern-keeping, was a natural target in a deeply patriarchal society. She had been accused before but was cleared of charges; however, in the new climate of fear, past suspicions were reignited.

The village minister, Samuel Parris, played a significant role in fanning the flames of paranoia. His sermons and public statements reinforced the belief that the Devil was actively working through certain members of the community, and that only by rooting them out could the colony survive. Parris's own niece, Abigail Williams, was one of the original afflicted girls, and her accusations carried a significant weight as well.

By the spring of 1692, the situation had escalated to such a degree that more than 30 people had been formally accused, and the jail cells in Salem and neighboring towns were rapidly filling up. The sheer number of arrests created an overwhelming sense of fear, not just of the accused witches, but of being accused oneself. People who might have once defended their neighbors now remained silent, terrified that speaking up could place a target on their own backs.

As the accusations continued to spread, they began to reach individuals who had little or no connection to

Salem Village itself. In this way, the witch hunt expanded beyond local disputes and became a colony-wide crisis. This frenzy of arrests and accusations marked the beginning of a legal process that would ultimately lead to one of the darkest chapters in colonial American history, as the trials themselves began to take shape.

The journey from suspicion to arrest in Salem was a rapid and dangerous one, driven by fear, social tension, and an ever-growing list of grievances. What had begun as the afflictions of a few girls had, within a matter of weeks, enveloped an entire community, pitting neighbor against neighbor in a desperate attempt to stave off an unseen, yet deeply feared, enemy.

The Court of Oyer and Terminer

The Court of Oyer and Terminer was established in 1692, in the midst of the chaos and fear that had overtaken Salem and its surrounding towns. With accusations of witchcraft spiraling out of control, the colonial government recognized that it needed a special court to manage the growing number of cases. The court's name itself provides some insight into its function—derived from French, "oyer" means "to hear" and "terminer" means "to determine." Essentially, this was a court set up to hear accusations and determine the guilt or innocence of the accused.

The court was established by the acting governor of the Massachusetts Bay Colony, William Phips, who had only recently returned from England with his official commission. When he arrived back in Boston, he found that the witchcraft hysteria had already taken hold, and the colonial legal system was unable to cope with the sheer number of accusations. Phips quickly issued a commission for a special court to be formed in Salem to try the alleged witches.

One of the most significant figures in this court was William Stoughton, a stern and uncompromising man who served as the chief judge. Stoughton was not only a judge but also the lieutenant governor of the colony, and he wielded tremendous influence. A staunch believer in the reality of witchcraft, he approached the trials with a sense of moral certainty, convinced that rooting out witches was a divine mission. His unyielding nature would become a driving force behind the court's harsh and, at times, dubious proceedings.

The structure of the Court of Oyer and Terminer reflected the urgency of the situation. While courts of this type were not uncommon in English law—often convened to address particularly pressing or overwhelming legal matters—this one was unique in its focus on witchcraft. It was composed of judges selected from among the colony's political and legal elite. Alongside Stoughton were several other prominent figures, including Samuel Sewall, John Hathorne, and Jonathan Corwin. Hathorne and Corwin had already been involved in early examinations of accused witches and were known for their particularly aggressive interrogation techniques.

Unlike standard colonial trials, which adhered more closely to English legal traditions, the Court of Oyer and Terminer operated under a different set of principles, largely shaped by the hysteria and fear of the time. One of the most glaring departures from standard legal practices was the court's reliance on "spectral evidence." This type of evidence—testimony that the spirit or specter of the accused had been seen committing acts of witchcraft—was highly controversial even in its own time. In traditional English courts, spectral evidence was considered dubious at best, as it could not be corroborated by any physical proof. Nevertheless, in Salem, it became a cornerstone of the prosecution's case. Witnesses, often young girls who had been swept up in the hysteria, would claim to see the specters of the accused tormenting them, and this testimony was frequently enough to secure a conviction.

The use of spectral evidence, along with the acceptance of "witch marks"—blemishes or moles on the body that were believed to be signs of a pact with the devil—set the trials apart from standard legal proceedings. These deviations from the norm were fueled by the court's sense of urgency and a belief that they were dealing with an existential threat to the community. The judges, led by Stoughton, believed that witchcraft represented a direct assault on the moral and spiritual fabric of the colony, and they were willing to bend traditional legal rules to eradicate it.

Another way in which the court diverged from typical legal practices was the absence of legal representation for the accused. In a normal trial, defendants would have had the right to counsel, and a more rigorous standard of evidence would have been required for conviction. But in the Court of Oyer and Terminer, the accused witches were often left to defend themselves, with little to no legal guidance. Many of the accused were poor, uneducated, and terrified, facing a court that was predisposed to believe in their guilt. This lack of a proper defense, combined with the emotional fervor of the trials, made it nearly impossible for the accused to present a coherent or persuasive case for their innocence.

The procedures of the court were swift and unforgiving. Once a person was accused, they would be brought before the court to stand trial, often in a matter of days. The trials themselves were short, sometimes lasting only a few hours. The judges would listen to the testimony of accusers—typically young girls who claimed to be afflicted by witchcraft—and would then interrogate the accused, often using leading or aggressive questions designed to elicit a confession. In many cases, the accused were pressured into confessing to save their own lives, as those who confessed were often spared execution, while those who maintained their innocence were more likely to be hanged.

The overall atmosphere of the court was one of moral panic. The judges, steeped in the Puritan belief that the devil was actively working to undermine their godly community, saw the accused witches as agents of evil. This worldview encompasses every aspects of the trials, from the evidence they accepted to the sentences they handed down. The court's purpose was not merely to administer justice in a legal sense but to protect the community from what they believed was a very real spiritual threat.

The establishment of the Court of Oyer and Terminer marked a pivotal moment in the Salem witch trials. It institutionalized the agitation and gave it a legal framework, allowing the fears of the community to be funneled into a formal process that, indirectly, only intensified the panic. By the time the court was dissolved in October 1692, 19 people had been executed, and the colony was beginning to question the legitimacy of the trials.

In retrospect, the court's procedures and rulings stand as a stark example of how fear can warp the legal system and lead to grave injustices. The acceptance of spectral evidence, the lack of proper legal representation, and the overall atmosphere of uncertainty all contributed to a legal process that was deeply flawed. However, in the moment, the judges and community believed they were doing what was necessary to safeguard their society from a malevolent force. The Court of Oyer and Terminer, for all its legal and moral failings, offers a chilling lesson in how quickly the rule of law can be subverted in the face of fear and superstition.

Spectral Evidence: The Invisible Threat

The Salem witch trials of 1692 are often characterized by their reliance on an unusual form of proof known as spectral evidence. This concept, pivotal to the proceedings, referred to testimony that the spirit or specter of a person was seen committing witchcraft, even if the accused was physically miles away. Understanding spectral evidence provides crucial insight into the fears and social dynamics that fueled the trials, revealing how a blend of superstition, theology, and legal ambiguity allowed this intangible proof to wield immense power in colonial Massachusetts.

Spectral evidence is defined as testimony that an accused witch's spirit appeared to the witness in a vision or dream and engaged in malevolent acts. Unlike physical evidence, which could be tested or scrutinized, spectral evidence existed solely in the realm of the unseen. This made it particularly troubling and fascinating, as it invoked a profound sense of fear and paranoia in a community already stricken by anxiety over the unknown.

For example, during the trials, several young girls, including Abigail Williams and Ann Putnam Jr., claimed to experience visions in which they saw the specters of various accused witches tormenting them. These claims were often accompanied by dramatic displays of distress, making them compelling in the eyes of the court. The testimonies of these young witnesses became a cornerstone of the prosecution's case, leading to the conviction and execution of numerous individuals based solely on these claims.

Theological and Legal Debates

The use of spectral evidence sparked significant theological and legal debates among the judges, clergy, and townspeople. At the heart of these discussions was a fundamental question: could the devil indeed manifest his influence through the specters of the accused? Puritan beliefs held that the devil was actively seeking to undermine the community by using witches as his agents. This perspective lent credence to the idea that spectral evidence was not only valid but essential in identifying those who had made pacts with evil.

However, some voices within the community, including respected figures like Increase Mather, raised objections. Mather cautioned against the use of spectral evidence, arguing that it could lead to false accusations and wrongful convictions. He famously stated, "It is a very dangerous thing to admit the testimony of specters." This tension between fervent belief in the supernatural and the principles of justice reflected the broader struggle between faith and reason that characterized the era.

Persuasiveness to Judges and Juries

The allure of spectral evidence lay in its ability to exploit the fears and uncertainties of the time. In a society grappling with issues such as disease, economic hardship, and shifting social structures, the idea that invisible forces could wreak havoc resonated deeply. This fear was compounded by the Puritan belief in original sin and the pervasive notion of an omnipresent evil, making spectral evidence appear not only plausible but necessary for protecting the community.

Judges and juries were often swayed by the emotional testimonies of those claiming to be afflicted. The dramatic accounts of spectral encounters created a narrative that was difficult to contest. When a witness declared that she had seen the specter of an accused witch afflicting her, it was hard for jurors to dismiss the claim, especially in a context where spiritual warfare was considered a daily reality. The fear of the unseen became a powerful motivator, leading to a collective willingness to accept intangible proof over more concrete evidence.

Additionally, the reliance on personal narratives in the aspects revealed the human tendency to trust emotional resonance over empirical evidence. In the Salem trials, the visceral reactions of the accusers played a crucial role in shaping public perception and judicial outcomes, much like how sensationalized stories can dominate headlines today.

Thus, spectral evidence played a critical role in the Salem witch trials, symbolizing the intersection of fear, faith, and the struggle for justice in a turbulent time. Its significance lies not only in its impact on the trials themselves but also in what it reveals about the human psyche—our susceptibility to fear, our desire for certainty in uncertain times, and the lengths we will go to protect our communities from perceived threats.

CHAPTER 3

Key Figures in the Trials

The Accusers: Abigail Williams and Her Circle

Abigail Williams, an orphaned niece of Reverend Samuel Parris, is often seen as the catalyst of the Salem Witch Trials, with her name forever tied to one of the darkest chapters in American colonial history. Only 11 years old at the time, her youth and seemingly uncontrollable outbursts of hysteria sparked the initial wave of panic that gripped Salem. Yet, while she is the most infamous accuser, she was not alone. A group of other young women and girls joined her, forming a circle of accusers whose testimonies were instrumental in sending many to their deaths.

Abigail was living in the household of her uncle, Reverend Samuel Parris, a strict and self-righteous minister who had come to Salem Village just a few years prior. The Parris household was itself a pressure cooker of religious fervor and domestic instability. Abigail had lost her parents during Native American raids on the Maine frontier, and this traumatic experience likely left her with lingering feelings of fear and anger, emotions which would later find an outlet during the trials. Living under the strict supervision of Reverend Parris must have intensified her sense of isolation and powerlessness. In early 1692, when she and her cousin Betty Parris began to experience strange fits—screaming, contorting, and claiming to see visions of spectral figures—the community was quick to assume that the devil was at work.

Abigail's circle consisted primarily of other young girls and teenagers from Salem Village, many of whom were similarly constrained by the rigid societal expectations of Puritan life. One of the most significant members was Ann Putnam Jr., the 12-year-old daughter of Thomas and Ann Putnam, a prominent family in the village. The Putnams had longstanding grievances with various members of the community, and it has been suggested that Ann's accusations were influenced, at least in part, by the desire to settle old scores. Thomas Putnam, in particular, was quick to file complaints on behalf of his daughter, suggesting a family-wide involvement in shaping the accusations. Ann Jr. accused over sixty people of witchcraft during the trials, making her one of the most prolific accusers. Her motivations may have been a mixture of genuine belief, family pressure, and a desire for attention in a community where children, especially girls, had little voice.

Another prominent figure was Elizabeth Hubbard, a 17-year-old servant in the household of Dr. William Griggs, the physician who initially diagnosed the girls' fits as being caused by witchcraft. Hubbard's role as a servant likely placed her in a subordinate position in society, and the trials gave her an unprecedented opportunity to wield power. As an accuser, she testified against 29 people, and her accusations were often dramatic and vivid. For instance, she claimed that Giles Corey, one of the eventual victims of the trials, had appeared to her as a spectral form, attempting to crush her under his weight. The psychological thrill of having her words taken seriously in a court of law, coupled with the intense social pressures she faced, might have fueled her participation.

Mercy Lewis, another key accuser, was also deeply affected by trauma. Like Abigail, she had lost her parents in violent frontier conflicts. Mercy was a servant in the household of the Putnams and had close ties to Ann Putnam Jr. Her accusations were often aligned with those of her mistress, suggesting that the Putnam family may have played a significant role in shaping her testimony. Mercy's experiences of violence and displacement on the frontier likely left her with unresolved psychological scars, and the witch trials provided a way to express her inner turmoil in a socially sanctioned manner.

The motivations of Abigail Williams and her circle are complex and cannot be reduced to a single cause. Fear, trauma, social pressures, and even boredom may have all played a role in their actions. In Puritan Salem, the lives of young girls were highly restricted. They were expected to remain obedient, pious, and silent, with few opportunities for self-expression. The witch trials gave them a chance to break free from these constraints, even if only temporarily. For the first time, these young girls had the undivided attention of the entire community, and their words carried the power to destroy lives. It's easy to imagine the intoxicating sense of control this might have given them, especially in a society where they were otherwise powerless.

Psychologically, the girls' behavior could be understood through the lens of mass hysteria, a phenomenon in which a group of people experience similar physical or emotional symptoms, often triggered by stress or fear. The rigid religious environment of Salem, combined with the daily threats of disease, war, and economic hardship, created a fertile ground for such hysteria to take root.

The girls may have initially experienced genuine physical symptoms—twitching, contorting, and experiencing visions—brought on by the stress of their environment. But once these symptoms were attributed to witchcraft, a kind of feedback loop was created, in which the girls' behavior was reinforced by the attention and validation they received from the community.

Abigail Williams, in particular, seemed to revel in her newfound power. During the trials, she accused several prominent members of the community, including the well-respected Rebecca Nurse and John Proctor. Her accusations were often accompanied by dramatic performances in the courtroom—she would scream, writhe on the floor, and claim to be attacked by the invisible specters of the accused. In one memorable instance, she accused Mary Warren, a former friend and fellow accuser, of witchcraft after Mary began to show signs of recanting her earlier testimony. Abigail's ability to turn on her former allies suggests a calculating aspect to her behavior, as if she understood the power dynamics at play and was willing to manipulate them to maintain her influence.

While it is easy to portray Abigail and the other accuser as villains, it's important to remember that they were children and teenagers operating in a highly repressive and terrifying environment. The pressures they faced—whether from their families, their community, or their own psychological trauma—were immense. Their accusations, though devastating in their consequences, were likely a product of the fear and uncertainty that permeated their world. They were both victims and perpetrators, caught up in a wave of hysteria that they helped create but could not control.

Eventually, Abigail Williams and her circle left an indelible mark on history, their actions leading to the deaths of 20 innocent people and the destruction of countless lives. Yet, their motivations remain a haunting mystery, a complex tangle of fear, power, and human frailty that continues to fascinate and disturb us centuries later.

The Judges: John Hathorne and Jonathan Corwin

The Salem witch trials are often remembered for the terrifying accusations and the fate of the accused, but much of the process rested in the hands of the judges who presided over these infamous trials. Among the most notable were John Hathorne and Jonathan Corwin. They weren't just men of law; they embodied the prevailing fear, religious zeal, and the weight of their Puritan convictions. To understand their role in these trials, one must first delve into their lives, judicial styles, and the legacy they left behind.

Born in 1641 in Salem, John Hathorne was a man who rose to prominence as a merchant and military officer before taking on the role of judge. A firm believer in the Puritan way of life, Hathorne was deeply rooted in the theological mindset of the time, which saw the devil's hand in many of life's misfortunes. By 1692, when the witch trials began, he was already a respected figure in Salem's elite circles, known for his strong, unyielding personality.

Hathorne's judicial approach during the Salem trials was driven by an almost fanatical belief in the righteousness of his cause. Unlike some of the more skeptical judges,

"Do you dare lie before God? The devil cannot hide in the face of righteousness. Look into my eyes and speak the truth. Have you made a covenant with the devil?" Hathorne's glare intensifies, his fists clenched on the bench.

Bridget looks down for a moment, overwhelmed by the pressure, and the courtroom erupts into gasps. *"See! She hesitates!"* Hathorne announces triumphantly. *"The truth of her wickedness is revealed!"*

This sort of direct confrontation was a hallmark of Hathorne's method. He believed that guilt manifested physically, whether in hesitation, trembling, or a mere glance away. He had little patience for ambiguity or nuance, making his role in these trials particularly devastating for the accused.

Historians over time have largely viewed Hathorne as emblematic of the dangers of blind zeal. His rigid Puritan beliefs, combined with an almost theatrical need to uncover guilt, have cast him as one of the more notorious figures of the Salem witch trials. His direct descendants, most notably the writer Nathaniel Hawthorne, would later distance themselves from his legacy. Nathaniel even changed the spelling of his last name to disassociate from the man whose actions he found shameful.

Jonathan Corwin: The Silent Authority

In contrast to the fiery Hathorne, Jonathan Corwin was a quieter, more reserved figure, but no less significant in his role. Born into a wealthy Salem family in 1640, Corwin was known as a man of status and influence. Before the trials, he had served in various local government roles and was a successful merchant. His home, now known as the "Witch House," still stands today as a symbol of his involvement in the witch trials.

Corwin's judicial approach was more methodical than Hathorne's. Where Hathorne would pounce with accusations and emotion, Corwin maintained a colder, more detached demeanor. He let the evidence—or what was presented as evidence—speak for itself, quietly guiding the trials from the shadows. His silence was often more intimidating than outright aggression, as he gave little indication of his thoughts or feelings on a case. This aloofness gave him an air of mystery and authority, which helped solidify his position as a key figure in Salem's judiciary during the trials.

In key cases, such as that of Rebecca Nurse, Corwin's involvement was significant. Nurse, a respected elderly woman, stood accused of witchcraft, and her trial became a turning point for many in Salem. Initially acquitted, she was retried after the afflicted girls claimed new evidence of her guilt. Corwin, who had not been overtly aggressive in her initial trial, let the second trial unfold with little intervention, allowing hysteria and the testimony of the accusers to overpower any reasoned defense.

Scene:

The trial of Rebecca Nurse, Corwin seated at the bench, observing the testimony of the afflicted girls.

One of the girls, writhing on the floor, suddenly points at Nurse, "She's pinching me! She sends her spirit to torment me!"

Rebecca Nurse, shocked, pleads with the court, "I *]* done nothing to harm these children. Please, innocent."

Corwin watches with a blank expression, oc nodding as if the truth was undeniable. Th silence falls over the room as he speaks: " heard the evidence. We shall proceed."

Corwin's ability to maintain a calm, measured demeanor only added to the sense of legitimacy that surrounded the trials. Yet historians have not looked upon him kindly. His refusal to question the validity of the spectral evidence or challenge the obvious manipulation of the afflicted girls has painted him as complicit in the tragic events. While he may not have been as outspoken as Hathorne, his passivity enabled the trials to spiral out of control.

Legacy and Historical Perspectives

Both Hathorne and Corwin played pivotal roles in the Salem witch trials, though their approaches differed. Hathorne's aggressive interrogation methods and Corwin's more subdued authority created a deadly combination of fear and indifference. Historians have long debated whether they truly believed in the guilt of the accused or if they were swept up in the hysteria of the time. Over the centuries, they've come to symbolize the dangers of unchecked power, blind faith, and a legal system that failed its people.

For Hathorne, his legacy is marred by his refusal to show mercy or doubt, a figure who pursued the accused with a fervor that bordered on the fanatical. Corwin, on the other hand, is often remembered for his silence—his refusal to question or intervene when justice was so obviously being perverted.

Together, they are part of the dark chapter of Salem's history, where justice was lost in the shadows of fear.

THE CLERGY: COTTON MATHER AND SAMUEL PARRIS

Cotton Mather and Samuel Parris were two of the most prominent clergymen involved in the Salem Witch Trials, but they played strikingly different roles in the hysteria that unfolded in 1692. Their theological views on witchcraft, their writings, and their influence on the trials provide a window into the religious fervor of colonial Massachusetts. Both men were deeply concerned with the spiritual health of their communities, but their approaches and legacies diverged sharply.

Samuel Parris, the minister of Salem Village, was at the heart of the trials from the very beginning. His household was the epicenter of the initial outbreak of supposed witchcraft. His daughter Betty and niece Abigail Williams were among the first to exhibit strange symptoms, and it was Parris who began to question whether witchcraft was at play. Parris's theological views were intensely rigid and steeped in the Puritan belief that Satan was a constant, active threat in the world. He preached often about the dangers of the Devil's influence, warning his congregation that Satan could manifest through witchcraft. This fear, combined with his precarious position as the minister of a divided and often contentious village, made Parris eager to find scapegoats for the misfortunes afflicting his congregation.

In his sermons during the trials, Parris emphasized the need for vigilance against Satan's forces. He described the afflicted girls' symptoms as clear signs of Satan's work. Parris's fervor contributed to an atmosphere where accusations were easily accepted and even encouraged. His stance on the matter can be gleaned from his sermons, where he proclaimed, "We are blind to Satan's devices, and too easily forget that he seeks to deceive the very elect." For Parris, the witch trials were a necessary purging of evil from the community, and he saw himself as playing a divine role in this moral cleansing.

Cotton Mather, on the other hand, was not directly involved in the early stages of the Salem trials but soon became one of its most influential commentators. A well-known minister and intellectual from Boston, Mather was fascinated by the supernatural and wrote extensively about demonic possession and witchcraft. His most famous work related to the trials is Wonders of the Invisible World, where he defended the trials and the judges but also showed a more cautious attitude than Parris. While Mather believed that witchcraft was real and that it needed to be eradicated, he also expressed concerns about the reliability of spectral evidence— testimony that accused witches' spirits or specters had appeared to the afflicted. He warned that such evidence was difficult to verify and could lead to false accusations.

In Wonders of the Invisible World, Mather wrote, *"It was apparent and most probable that evil angels came and accomplished these things, but the witches could never accomplish them themselves."* He acknowledged the existence of witchcraft but subtly questioned whether all of the accused were guilty of it. In contrast to Parris, who seemed consumed by the immediate need to identify witches, Mather was more concerned with how the trials reflected on the Puritan mission. For Mather, the trials were not merely a local affair; they were part of a broader spiritual battle. His writings tried to balance the need to combat Satan with the fear of unjust persecution, a balance that Parris rarely achieved.

Parris's role in the trials damaged his reputation significantly. Although he had initially gained the support of some of Salem Village's more devout Puritans, by the end of the trials, his reputation was in tatters. The increasing number of accusations, many of them targeting respected members of the community, eventually turned people against him. As the trials spiraled out of control, Parris's hardline stance became a liability. By 1694, Salem Village had had enough, and Parris was forced to leave his position as minister. His involvement in the trials effectively ended his career, and he spent the rest of his life in relative obscurity, moving from town to town, never again holding a stable pastoral position.

Mather's reputation, on the other hand, was more complex. In the years immediately following the trials, he remained a respected figure, but as public sentiment turned against the trials, so too did the view of his role in them. Though he had not been a judge or a prosecutor, his writings had lent intellectual and theological support to the proceedings. In later years, critics would point to

Mather's defense of the trials as evidence of his complicity in the tragedy. His legacy, however, was more enduring than Parris's. Mather continued to be an influential figure in New England, writing on a wide variety of subjects, from science to theology. His involvement in the trials, while a blemish on his career, did not ruin him as it did Parris.

In comparing these two figures, it is clear that while both were motivated by a genuine belief in the existence of witchcraft and the threat of Satan, their approaches were very different. Parris was a local figure, deeply embedded in the immediate panic and desperate to prove his worth to a divided community. His rigid theology and personal involvement in the events made him a central player, but it also led to his downfall. Mather, on the other hand, was more of an intellectual observer. His writings show a man concerned with the broader implications of the trials for Puritan society, even as he struggled with the ethical issues they raised.

Theologically, Parris leaned more heavily into the idea that witchcraft was an immediate and pressing danger that needed to be rooted out, regardless of the consequences. Mather, while still firmly believing in the reality of witchcraft, was more cautious and willing to entertain the possibility of mistakes being made. This difference in perspective is crucial to understanding their roles in the trials and the lasting impact they had. Parris's legacy is that of a man whose zeal helped fuel one of the darkest chapters in American history. Mather, while not free from blame, left a more complex legacy as a scholar who wrestled with the moral dilemmas of his time.

Their writings, sermons, and actions during the trials offer us not just a glimpse into the hysteria of Salem but into the broader anxieties of a society grappling with the presence of evil in a new world. Through their contrasting roles, It could be seen how religion, fear, and power intersected to create an atmosphere ripe for tragedy.

CHAPTER 4

The Accused: Faces of the Hunted

Bridget Bishop: First to the Gallows

Bridget Bishop's story begins long before the terror of the Salem Witch Trials gripped colonial Massachusetts. She was born in England around 1632, Bishop had already lived through several hardships by the time she was accused of witchcraft. She had been married three times and was known for her independent, outspoken nature—qualities that made her stand out in a society where women were expected to be submissive and modest. Her ownership of a tavern and a reputation for wearing brightly colored clothes, especially red, further marked her as different, if not entirely respectable by Puritan standards.

Bishop lived in Salem Town, not far from the bustling port. Her life was filled with the ordinary tasks of a woman trying to make her way in a community suspicious of anyone who didn't conform to strict religious and social norms. Her home was said to be filled with gatherings that included drinking and gambling—activities frowned upon by the deeply religious Puritan society. Bishop's tavern was a space where rules were bent, and it seems she, too, did not fit the mold of what a proper Puritan woman should be.

In 1692, when whispers of witchcraft spread from Salem Village to the surrounding areas, Bridget Bishop was among the first to be accused. Why her? Perhaps it was her independent spirit, her refusal to bow to the expectations of her gender, or the longstanding suspicion that had dogged her for years. She had been accused of witchcraft before, in 1680, but had been acquitted due to a lack of evidence. Still, the charges had left a stain, and in a community already primed to see the devil at work, those past accusations made her an easy target.

The specific charges against her in 1692 were serious and damning. Bishop was accused of afflicting five young women with fits, strange visions, and bodily harm. The court records paint a vivid picture: "Bridget Bishop, being indicted for not having the fear of God before her eyes and being seduced by the devil, and by his instigation, wickedly, maliciously, and feloniously, sundry times committed witchcraft." Witnesses claimed that she appeared to them as a specter, tormenting them with pinches and pricks. One testified that she had appeared in his bedroom at night, and another claimed that after a quarrel with Bishop, his child fell ill with strange fits.

The courtroom as a result of these accusations, syddenly became tensed. The atmosphere was thick with fear and anticipation as Bridget stood before the judges. The magistrates were eager to see justice served and were already steeped in the belief that the devil was at work in their town. Bishop's demeanor—described as defiant and bold—did little to help her case. She did not weep or beg, nor did she fit the image of a meek, penitent sinner. Her defiance was interpreted as a sign of guilt.

The evidence presented against her was largely spectral, meaning the afflicted claimed to see her spirit tormenting them while her physical body was elsewhere. In today's terms, this might seem flimsy, but to the Puritans, it was as real as any physical wound. One of the most damning pieces of evidence came in the form of a supposed poppet—an effigy used in witchcraft—which was found in her home. Though Bishop denied any knowledge of it, the very presence of such an object in her home was enough to confirm the fears of those already convinced of her guilt.

As the trial progressed, it became clear that Bridget Bishop was fighting a battle she could not win. Her past, her outspoken nature, and her connection to activities deemed immoral by Puritan standards were enough to paint her as a witch in the eyes of the court. Her conviction was swift. The jury found her guilty of witchcraft, and her fate was sealed.

On June 10, 1692, Bridget Bishop became the first person hanged during the Salem Witch Trials. Her execution set a grim precedent for what was to come. The gallows, hastily erected on Proctor's Ledge, stood as a stark reminder of the consequences of stepping outside societal norms. Witnesses to her death described the scene in chilling detail: the creaking of the wooden structure, the rough-hewn rope, the murmurs of the crowd, and finally, the terrible silence as her body went still. The hot June sun beat down on the gathered townspeople as they watched her life ebb away, their fear of the devil momentarily soothed by the sacrifice of another human being.

But why was Bridget Bishop the first? Her case, more than others, seemed to confirm the worst fears of the Puritans. She was everything a "witch" might be: independent, outspoken, and tied to activities like drinking and gambling that were associated with moral corruption. The court needed a quick conviction to validate the growing hysteria, and Bishop, with her past accusations and suspicious behavior, was an easy target. Her case set the tone for the trials to follow. The use of spectral evidence, the emphasis on reputation and community standing, and the swift nature of the proceedings would become hallmarks of the witch trials.

The story of Bridget Bishop is tragic, not just because of her unjust death but because of what it represented: the breakdown of reason in the face of fear. Her life, filled with the complexities of a woman navigating a restrictive society, was reduced to a few accusations and a rope. Yet, in death, she became a symbol—both of the horror of the Salem Witch Trials and of the countless women throughout history who have been punished for defying societal norms.

Bridget Bishop's case opened the floodgates. After her execution, the trials continued in full force, with more and more people—many of them women—being accused, tried, and executed. Her death was not the end, but the beginning of one of the darkest chapters in American history. Even today, her story serves as a haunting reminder of the dangers of hysteria and unchecked power.

Eventually, Bridget Bishop's defiance in life may have hastened her downfall, but it also left a lasting impression. Her refusal to conform, her independence, and her strength made her stand out in a world that feared such traits. And while that world condemned her for it, history remembers her as more than just the first victim of the Salem Witch Trials. She was a woman who lived on her own terms, even in the face of unimaginable injustice.

REBECCA NURSE: PIETY MEETS PREJUDICE

Rebecca Nurse was a beacon of piety in Salem, a figure respected by many for her devout nature and moral integrity. Born in 1621 in Great Yarmouth, England, she and her family immigrated to Massachusetts in the mid-1630s, settling in Salem Village. By all accounts, Nurse lived an exemplary life. She was a mother of eight children, a dedicated wife to her husband Francis, and a woman deeply rooted in the Puritan faith. Her family had gained moderate wealth and respect through their successful farm, and Rebecca was often described as a woman of profound virtue and religious devotion.

At the age of 71, Nurse was no stranger to the wear and tear of time. She was hard of hearing, likely suffering from the ailments of old age. Yet, despite her age and standing, she became one of the most shocking targets of the Salem witch trials. The accusation against her stunned the community. How could such a respected, elderly matron, a stalwart of religious and community life, find herself branded a witch?

The Context of Rebecca Nurse's Accusation

The accusations against Nurse arose in early 1692, in a climate of escalating paranoia. Salem had already seen a handful of women, many of lower social standing, accused of witchcraft. But Rebecca Nurse was different. Her piety and position in the community should have shielded her from such suspicions. The initial charge against her was made by Edward and John Putnam, relatives of Thomas Putnam, a key figure in driving the witch hunt. The Nurse family had long been at odds with the Putnam family over land disputes, leading some to believe that these tensions played a role in her accusation.

Her frailty and old age only heightened the absurdity of the accusations. *"What, do these people think I am an innocent child, to be led into such wickedness?"* Nurse exclaimed when she first heard of the accusations, her disbelief clear from the historical record. But in the frenzy of Salem's witch hunt, reason and logic had little place. Despite her spotless reputation, Nurse's fate was sealed by fear, jealousy, and a legal system more concerned with proving guilt than finding truth.

Rebecca Nurse's Trial

Rebecca Nurse's trial was, in many ways, a spectacle. She stood accused of "sundry acts of witchcraft," primarily based on the testimony of the "afflicted girls," including Abigail Williams, Ann Putnam Jr., and Mercy Lewis. They claimed that Nurse had tormented them with specters, causing them intense physical and spiritual pain. As she stood in the courtroom, these girls would go into fits, screaming and contorting their bodies, allegedly at the sight of her spirit.

The trial, held in June 1692, was marked by both drama and deeply held prejudices. Nurse's advanced age and her hearing difficulties often left her confused and unable to follow the accusations. Her dignity and religious piety, however, were evident throughout the trial. She maintained her innocence, relying on her faith and the truth she believed would ultimately set her free. Her family and neighbors spoke in her defense, providing testimonies of her good character. Yet, as with so many of the accused, the tide of superstition and fear was overwhelming.

In an extraordinary moment, the jury initially found her not guilty. This verdict should have ended her ordeal, but the courtroom atmosphere was volatile. The afflicted girls fell into fits, loudly protesting the decision. Judge Stoughton, sensing the tension, pressured the jury to reconsider. One juror later testified that Rebecca Nurse's ambiguous response to a question had cast doubt on her innocence, though it was more likely a misunderstanding due to her hearing difficulties. Ultimately, the jury reversed its decision, delivering a guilty verdict.

When Nurse heard of the reversal, she was devastated. In a letter to the court, she wrote: *"These actions indeed were by me said, but not in that sense as they are now put. God knows I am innocent."* The weight of the false conviction, compounded by the court's disregard for her testimony, broke her spirit. Despite petitions from her family and neighbors, Governor Phips, under pressure from the court and public, refused to intervene.

A Case of Injustice

Rebecca Nurse's trial is often cited as one of the clearest examples of the deep injustice and irrationality that characterized the Salem witch trials. It revealed how even the most respected members of the community were not safe from accusations and how fear and hysteria could erode the very foundations of justice. Nurse's piety should have been her defense, but in a society gripped by religious extremism and paranoia, it became an ironic twist in her downfall.

The overturning of the not guilty verdict highlights the extent to which the legal process had become corrupted by the pressures of public opinion and the manipulations of those in power. It demonstrated that the trials were not about determining guilt or innocence but about satisfying the communal need for scapegoats.

Nurse's case also reflected the broader prejudices of the time. As a woman in her seventies, Rebecca was seen as vulnerable to the Devil's influence, her age and gender making her an easy target in a society that equated female vulnerability with spiritual weakness. Historian Carol Karlsen has argued that the witch trials often targeted women who did not conform to societal expectations, particularly those who were older, independent, or outspoken. While Rebecca Nurse was known for her piety, the fact that she had been involved in a long-standing dispute with the influential Putnam family likely contributed to her being singled out. It was a dangerous combination of personal vendettas, religious fanaticism, and gendered suspicion.

The Execution and Legacy

On July 19, 1692, Rebecca Nurse was executed by hanging on Gallows Hill. Her composure in the face of death further cemented her status as a martyr in the eyes of many. One contemporary account noted, "When she was executed, she went as composed as any person under such circumstances might." The dignity with which she faced her unjust execution left a lasting impression on those who believed in her innocence.

In the years following the trials, as public opinion shifted and the true horror of the events came to light, Rebecca Nurse's name was among those exonerated. Her legacy endures as a symbol of the deep injustice of the Salem witch trials and the dangers of unchecked hysteria. A memorial now stands in Danvers, Massachusetts (formerly Salem Village), at the Rebecca Nurse

Homestead, a testament to her faith, courage, and the tragedy that befell an innocent woman.

Rebecca Nurse's case remains a powerful reminder of how fear, prejudice, and a desire for control can lead to the persecution of the most unlikely individuals. Her story, like many from the Salem trials, serves as both a cautionary tale and a solemn reflection on the capacity for human injustice.

John Proctor: A Skeptic's Fate

John Proctor was a man who didn't easily bend to superstition. A successful farmer in his mid-sixties, he had earned his way to a respected position in Salem society. His deep skepticism of the witchcraft hysteria that had overtaken the village set him apart, as did his outspokenness. In the spring of 1692, Proctor saw the growing frenzy for what it was: a dangerous mix of fear, religious fanaticism, and opportunism.

"He's a hard, stern man," the neighbors whispered. Proctor had made no secret of his disdain for the accusers, particularly for the young girls at the heart of the hysteria. "Foolishness," he would say with a shake of his head. To him, the fainting fits, the wild accusations—

it was all a farce, a dangerous game. "If they want a witch, let them come to me," he once sarcastically remarked, unknowingly sealing his fate.

His wife, Elizabeth, wasn't as vocal but shared his skepticism. She watched uneasily as the trials claimed one life after another, quietly supporting her husband's stance but with a growing sense of foreboding. Their world was changing, and even John's strength couldn't keep the madness from seeping into their lives.

It began in late March 1692, when Abigail Williams and Mary Walcott, two of the central accusers, claimed that Elizabeth's spirit had attacked them. John, livid, marched into the town and demanded the madness stop. "I'll bring you to your senses!" he reportedly shouted at the accusers. His boldness, however, had the opposite effect. Rather than quelling the storm, it placed the Proctors under closer scrutiny. By April, John himself was implicated in the growing web of accusations.

When John first heard that his name had been brought up, he scoffed. "They've lost their minds," he said to Elizabeth. But the accusations didn't stop. Witnesses came forward, claiming that Proctor's specter had tormented them. Some of the most damning testimonies came from the same girls he had openly mocked. "He came to me in the night," Abigail Williams cried, trembling before the magistrates. "He told me to sign the Devil's book!"

Proctor's response was to demand proof—tangible, physical evidence, not the spectral nonsense that had condemned so many. But in Salem's court, there was no such thing. Spectral evidence—testimonies of invisible spirits and unseen forces—was enough to condemn a person to death.

When John was formally arrested in April, his shock was palpable. *"Have we all gone mad?"* he reportedly said when the constables came to take him. His initial disbelief turned into steely resolve. *"I am no witch,"* he declared before the court. *"I am a plain farmer, a God-fearing Christian. You'll have no confession from me, for I have done nothing."*

But the court wanted more than denials. They wanted confessions. John, defiant as ever, refused to bend. He openly criticized the court, questioning the validity of the proceedings. *"These girls,"* he argued, *"are liars, feeding on each other's madness."* His outbursts only deepened the court's suspicion. How could a man who spoke so fiercely against the trials be anything but guilty?

The evidence against him was lacking accuracy, but in Salem, it mattered little. The accusers spoke of his specter tormenting them, and some of the villagers—whether out of fear, envy, or simple misjudgment—testified that he had a *"hard heart"* and that his anger was the work of the Devil. Even some of his own household staff, under pressure, turned against him. Mary Warren, a servant in the Proctor household who had been swept up in the hysteria, first defended her master, but under the court's gaze, she changed her tune. *"He made me sign the Devil's book,"* she tearfully confessed.

John's defense was fierce. He brought forward over 30 villagers who testified to his and Elizabeth's good character, but their voices were drowned out by the hysteria. In the face of mounting pressure, he stood firm. *"I will die before I confess to a lie,"* he said.

Proctor's trial was a turning point in the witch hunt for one key reason: he was a man. While most of the accused were women, Proctor's case showed that no one was safe, regardless of gender. His execution sent a chilling message—anyone who spoke out, anyone who questioned the legitimacy of the trials, could find themselves at the gallows.

In August of 1692, Proctor was sentenced to death. On the day of his execution, he walked to the gallows with a quiet dignity, refusing to beg for mercy or confess to a crime he did not commit. The heat of the summer sun beat down as the crowd gathered. *"I am no witch,"* he declared once more, standing before the noose. *"God knows I am innocent."* The words hung heavy in the air as the executioner did his grim work.

For those who knew John Proctor, his death was not just a tragedy but a symbol of the madness that had overtaken Salem. He had entered the trials as a skeptic, and even as the noose tightened around his neck, he remained unshaken in his disbelief. His legacy, however, would outlive him. Years after the hysteria died down, his case, along with others, became a rallying point for those who sought justice for the wrongly accused. His courage, particularly in standing up as a man during a time when women bore the brunt of the accusations, became a beacon of resistance.

In the years following the trials, some of the key figures who had condemned him publicly repented. In 1706, Ann

Putnam Jr., one of the original accusers, issued a public apology, admitting that she had been *"deluded by Satan"* in accusing innocent people, including the Proctors. But for John, that apology came far too late.

John Proctor's story is one of defiance, of standing firm in the face of irrational fear and religious extremism. He died not as a victim but as a man who, even in his final moments, refused to betray his own conscience. His fate reminds us that skepticism, though dangerous in times of hysteria, is often the strongest defense against the madness of the crowd.

CHAPTER 5

Beyond Salem: The Spread of Fear

Andover's Witch Hunt

The town of Andover, like Salem, found itself swept into the frenzy of witchcraft accusations in 1692. Located about 15 miles from Salem Village, Andover's involvement in the witch hunt was not an isolated incident but an extension of the hysteria that had already gripped much of colonial Massachusetts. The events that unfolded there, however, took on their own unique form, marked by a flood of accusations and confessions that set Andover apart from Salem.

It all began in July 1692 when members of Andover sought out the afflicted girls of Salem, asking for their assistance in identifying witches within their community. With the specter of witchcraft already looming large, the very presence of these accusers, who claimed to see the invisible world and its demonic inhabitants, fueled the fear that witchcraft was taking root in Andover as well. Once the accusations started, they spread like wildfire, with the first major wave implicating Ann Foster, an elderly widow with a reputation for strange behavior. Her interrogation, which was conducted with intense pressure, led to her confession of witchcraft, setting the tone for what would follow.

In contrast to Salem, where accusations were often fueled by personal grievances, in Andover, the pattern that emerged was driven largely by confessions. This distinctive feature may have been born out of the intense fear gripping the town. People, already terrified by the possibility of witchcraft, began confessing not only to avoid execution but also out of genuine belief that they were involved in some supernatural wrongdoing. The Andover confessions were particularly remarkable because many individuals admitted to witchcraft with little or no prompting. Once one person confessed, it seemed to open the floodgates. This created a ripple effect that left the community weak.

Among the key figures in Andover's witch hunt was Joseph Ballard, a local man whose wife was gravely ill. Ballard's suspicions that witchcraft was the cause of her illness were the catalyst for the Salem accusers' involvement in Andover. His invitation to the afflicted girls to help root out witches effectively brought the trials to the town's doorstep. His wife's illness, believed to be the result of a curse, pushed him to find a scapegoat, and the ensuing panic left nearly no one in Andover untouched by suspicion.

Ann Foster, one of the first to be accused in Andover, is a haunting example of how quickly the web of accusations could grow. Her initial confession did not end with herself; it led to her implicating her daughter, Mary Lacey, and later, her granddaughter, also named Mary Lacey. The three generations of women were jailed, creating a stark and tragic illustration of how families could be torn apart by the trials. Ann Foster's confession was particularly chilling in its detail. She spoke of riding on poles to witches' meetings and of participating in strange, diabolical ceremonies. Such vivid confessions provided fuel to the growing hysteria, offering supposed proof of the dark forces at work in the community.

The role of confessions in Andover marks a striking contrast with Salem, where many of the accused stubbornly denied the charges against them. In Salem, people like Rebecca Nurse, John Proctor, and Martha Corey stood firm in their innocence despite the overwhelming pressure to confess. Their steadfastness was seen as defiance and often led to harsher punishments. In Andover, however, the rampant confessions helped some to avoid the noose, though they did not escape the torment of imprisonment or the lifelong stigma of being associated with witchcraft. For many in Andover, confessing was a means of self-preservation, but it also fanned the flames of the hysteria, leading to more accusations.

Andover's witch hunt saw a particularly high number of accusations—around 40 people in a town much smaller than Salem. The sheer scale of the panic can be traced to a combination of factors. First, the involvement of the Salem accusers brought an external influence that quickly exacerbated local fears. Second, the culture of confession created a cycle in which one person's admission of guilt would prompt others to confess, often naming others in the process. Andover's residents, already frightened, may have felt compelled to name names to escape their fate. This cycle of accusation and confession spun rapidly, trapping many in its wake.

Another figure whose story reflects the unique nature of Andover's witch trials is Abigail Faulkner. She was a respectable woman from a prominent family, but even her status could not shield her from the rage. Accused of witchcraft, she eventually confessed under duress. Her confession, like many others, followed a common pattern: under the pressure of the questioning, she admitted to signing the devil's book and engaging in witchcraft. Faulkner's case is notable not only because of her social standing but also because she was pregnant at the time of her conviction. This allowed her to temporarily avoid execution, as pregnant women were often spared until after they had given birth. Nevertheless, Faulkner's confession and the public nature of her trial served as a powerful reminder that no one in Andover, regardless of status, was beyond the reach of the witch hunt.

The panic's impact on Andover was devastating. The constant fear of witchcraft and the oppressive atmosphere of suspicion tore the community apart. Families were pitted against each other, with relatives accusing one another in a desperate attempt to escape the trials. The widespread belief in witchcraft, stoked by both the accusers and the confessions, created a toxic environment in which reason and evidence were drowned out by hysteria.

Eventually, the events in Andover mirrored those in Salem in terms of their origins in fear and superstition, but they diverged in the way the witch hunt played out. While Salem became infamous for its dramatic trials and executions, Andover's story is one of widespread confessions and a feverish atmosphere of self-accusation. The trials in Andover didn't result in the same number of executions, but they left deep scars on the town's collective psyche. The confessions and accusations destroyed families, broke down trust within the community, and left a lingering sense of shame that would not soon be forgotten.

The case of Andover provides a sobering reflection on how the witchcraft hysteria could infiltrate even the most ordinary of communities, turning neighbors into accusers and leading to a breakdown of social order. It stands as a chilling example of how fear, once unleashed, can spread beyond its point of origin and take on a life of its own, leaving devastation in its wake.

Ipswich and Beverly: Resistance and Reason

In 1692, as the witchcraft hysteria tore through Salem Village and surrounding areas, nearby communities such as Ipswich and Beverly were swept up in the same anxiety. However, these towns displayed varying degrees of participation in the Salem Witch Trials, with some notable instances of resistance. By examining the local dynamics of Ipswich and Beverly, we can understand why these communities were not as deeply affected by the hysteria compared to Salem Village. Local leadership, resistance by figures such as Reverend John Wise, and a focus on reason over panic played key roles in creating a stark contrast between these towns and the epicenter of the trials.

Ipswich: The Role of Rationality and Resistance

Ipswich, located just north of Salem, experienced its own share of witchcraft accusations, but it did not spiral into the same level of chaos seen in Salem Village. One of the critical factors in Ipswich's relative calm during the witch trials was the role played by local leaders, especially Reverend John Wise. A Harvard-educated minister, Wise was an influential figure in Ipswich and well-known for his outspoken opposition to colonial authorities on several issues, including taxes and governance. When the witch trials began to gain momentum, Wise took a firm stance against the proceedings, arguing that the trials were an affront to reason and justice.

Wise's opposition to the trials reflected broader resistance within Ipswich to the growing hysteria. While some Ipswich residents were accused of witchcraft—such as Elizabeth Howe, who was eventually executed—the town did not descend into the mass accusations and neighborly betrayals that plagued Salem. Wise's emphasis on rationality and his criticism of the trials provided a moral anchor for the community, reminding people that the witchcraft accusations were rooted in fear rather than facts. This resistance to hysteria likely contributed to the more moderate response to the witch trials in Ipswich, where the town did not allow fear to completely overrun their sense of justice.

Beverly: A Town on the Periphery

Beverly, situated just south of Salem, also felt the effects of the witch trials but to a much lesser degree than its neighboring village. Beverly's close geographical proximity to Salem meant that it was not immune to the hysteria. Several Beverly residents were implicated in the witchcraft accusations, including Sarah Osborn, a widow accused of witchcraft in early 1692. However, Beverly, like Ipswich, avoided the overwhelming spread of panic.

One factor that may have helped Beverly stay somewhat removed from the frenzy was its more cautious leadership. Reverend John Hale, the minister of Beverly, initially supported the trials but later became one of its harshest critics after his own wife was accused of witchcraft. Hale's change of heart reflected a growing disillusionment with the legal and moral foundations of the trials. His eventual opposition to the witch hunt became an important voice of reason, helping to temper the spread of hysteria within Beverly.

Additionally, Beverly was a community that had strong internal cohesion. The town's relatively small size and tight-knit relationships among its residents may have made it more resistant to the factionalism and paranoia that took root in Salem Village. Rather than turning on one another in a panic-driven frenzy, Beverly's residents displayed more skepticism toward the witchcraft accusations. While the town was not entirely spared from the trials, it remained a place where reason and caution had a stronger influence than in Salem.

Contrasting Approaches: Salem vs. Ipswich and Beverly

In Salem, the trials were driven by intense social divisions, economic stress, and the strong influence of religious extremism, particularly from Reverend Samuel Parris, who fanned the flames of witchcraft hysteria. Parris's sermons frequently invoked the devil and played into the fears of his congregation, providing religious justification for the trials.

In contrast, Ipswich and Beverly had leaders like John Wise and John Hale, who approached the situation with more caution and, in Wise's case, outright resistance. While Reverend Hale initially supported the trials, his eventual repudiation of them showed a willingness to question the legitimacy of the accusations, particularly when they touched his own family. Wise's firm stance against the trials from the beginning demonstrated his commitment to rationality and justice, making him a key figure in resisting the spread of hysteria.

Moreover, the social dynamics in Ipswich and Beverly were not as fractured as those in Salem Village. Ipswich, in particular, had a more established and stable community structure, with less of the internal strife that marked Salem. The economic and political tensions that contributed to the witch trials in Salem were not as pronounced in these neighboring towns, which may have helped to curb the spread of witchcraft accusations. Without the same level of social anxiety and without a leader like Samuel Parris driving the hysteria forward, Ipswich and Beverly were able to maintain a greater sense of calm and reason.

John Wise: Resistance in Action

John Wise's opposition to the witch trials provides an important example of how resistance to mass hysteria can play a pivotal role in curbing its spread. Wise was no stranger to conflict with authority—he had previously clashed with the colonial government over taxation and the imposition of laws he saw as unjust. His dissenting nature made him one of the few public figures in the region to openly question the legitimacy of the witch trials.

Wise argued that the trials lacked proper legal grounding and that the evidence being used to convict the accused was flimsy at best. His focus on rationality and due process was a direct challenge to the emotional and fear-driven atmosphere that fueled the trials in Salem Village. Although Wise's resistance did not prevent the execution of individuals like Elizabeth Howe, his efforts contributed to a broader sense of skepticism about the trials in Ipswich.

Lessons in Leadership and Community

The experiences of Ipswich and Beverly during the Salem Witch Trials illustrate the critical importance of leadership, community cohesion, and resistance to mass hysteria. While these towns were not entirely spared from the witchcraft accusations, they managed to avoid the catastrophic social collapse that occurred in Salem Village. Leaders like John Wise and John Hale, through their rationality and eventual resistance, played key roles in tempering the spread of fear. The differences between these communities and Salem highlight how local dynamics—whether they be the influence of a single leader or the overall stability of a community—can profoundly affect the outcomes of events like the Salem Witch Trials.

By comparing Ipswich and Beverly with Salem, we see how reason and resistance can prevail over fear and hysteria, offering a powerful lesson in the importance of critical thinking and moral leadership during times of crisis.

The Ripple Effect in New England

The Salem witch trials of 1692 did not unfold in isolation. News of the trials spread across New England like wildfire, stirring reactions, anxieties, and debates throughout the region. While Massachusetts bore the brunt of the hysteria, the effects of the trials were felt across neighboring colonies, altering public opinion, shaping governance, and impacting the reputation of New England as a whole.

Immediate Reaction and Spread of News

The Salem witch trials were highly publicized, with letters, sermons, and official documents disseminating the grim details to other colonies. News from Salem spread quickly, partly because of the tight-knit nature of the New England colonies, which shared common social, political, and religious ties. The Puritans, who largely populated these colonies, viewed themselves as a united group, and events in one area were of great interest to those in others.

In the initial stages, many outside Massachusetts expressed shock but also curiosity. The religious leaders in the region, most of whom shared similar Puritan values, were eager to learn of the theological justifications for the trials. They believed, to some extent, that Massachusetts was carrying out a divine duty to root out witches. However, this early curiosity quickly shifted to concern as the scale of the accusations became known.

Copycat Accusations and Trials in Other Colonies

As news of the Salem trials spread, it inevitably led to similar events in other parts of New England. One such instance occurred in Andover, Massachusetts, just outside Salem. Though technically part of Massachusetts, the Andover cases illustrate how the hysteria bled beyond the original epicenter. In Andover, accusations spread like wildfire after a group of local women confessed under pressure to being witches, triggering a series of trials that resulted in multiple arrests.

Beyond Massachusetts, the neighboring colony of Connecticut had its own history of witch trials, but the events of 1692 in Salem reignited witchcraft fears. In Fairfield, Connecticut, accusations were made against Elizabeth Clawson and Mercy Disborough, both of whom were accused of witchcraft around the same time as the Salem trials. The Fairfield trials, although more restrained and ending with fewer executions, demonstrate the ripple effect that Salem had on neighboring colonies. While Connecticut had been more cautious, Salem's precedent provided fuel for continued suspicion.

In Rhode Island, there were fewer formal trials, but the uncertainty was evident. Rhode Island's more religiously diverse population—owing to its foundation as a haven for those seeking freedom from the strict Puritan orthodoxy of Massachusetts—meant that witchcraft accusations did not take the same form. Still, individuals accused of *"ungodly behavior"* found themselves scrutinized more intensely in the aftermath of Salem.

Even colonies farther afield, like New York, were influenced. Though witch trials in New York were infrequent compared to New England, the Salem hysteria spurred a few accusations in the region, as well as growing concern about the potential dangers of witchcraft. What became evident was that Salem's trials had a contagious quality, emboldening people in other colonies to voice long-held suspicions and grievances, often turning personal vendettas into witchcraft accusations.

Reactions from Colonial Leaders

As the witchcraft hysteria escalated in Salem, colonial leaders outside Massachusetts became increasingly alarmed. The spectacle of the trials raised concerns about governance, religious extremism, and social order. In Connecticut, leaders were notably more cautious, having already dealt with witch trials in earlier decades. The Fairfield trials, though influenced by Salem, showed a more restrained approach; Connecticut's leaders were wary of the excessive fervor that had gripped Massachusetts.

In Rhode Island, the government, under the leadership of men like Governor Samuel Cranston, was openly critical of the witch trials in Massachusetts. Rhode Island's more tolerant religious stance provided a stark contrast to the Puritan zeal in Salem. Leaders in the colony emphasized rational governance and warned against the dangers of religious extremism. This critical stance, along with Rhode Island's reputation for religious tolerance, helped the colony avoid the kinds of large-scale witch hunts seen in Massachusetts.

The influence of political and religious leaders was also felt in New York. Governor Benjamin Fletcher, who was governing the colony at the time, expressed deep reservations about the events in Salem. Although there were occasional accusations of witchcraft in New York, Fletcher ensured that they did not escalate into a full-blown witch hunt, likely learning from the chaos in Massachusetts.

Long-Term Impact on New England's Reputation

In the years following the Salem witch trials, New England's reputation took a noticeable hit, particularly in the eyes of other English colonies and authorities in London. Massachusetts had long been viewed as a stronghold of Puritan orthodoxy and moral rigor, but the trials exposed the darker side of this religious intensity. The widespread agitation, mass arrests, and public executions showed a colony unable to temper its religious zeal with reason.

For other colonies in New England, Salem became a cautionary tale. In Connecticut and Rhode Island, which had already experienced their own smaller-scale witch trials, the aftermath of 1692 led to increased skepticism about future accusations of witchcraft. Colonial leaders and religious figures became more cautious, and there was a growing sense that such trials were more destructive than beneficial.

The trials also had a chilling effect on religious extremism. For decades, the Puritans had governed with a heavy hand, blending religious and civil authority. However, the fallout from Salem revealed the dangers of unchecked theocratic rule. In the decades that followed, New England, especially Massachusetts, began to move towards more secular forms of governance, with greater separation between church and state.

The Lasting Legacy on Governance

In the wake of Salem, colonial governments across New England took steps to prevent such hysteria from occurring again. Massachusetts, in particular, underwent significant legal reforms. By the early 18th century, colonial leaders had introduced changes to the legal system that made it much harder for spectral evidence—the controversial testimony of seeing spirits or visions—to be admitted in court. These legal reforms reflected the growing consensus that reason and law, not religious zeal, should guide justice.

The Salem trials also had a broader impact on colonial governance by prompting increased oversight from England. The British Crown, already suspicious of the independent streak in the Massachusetts colony, took a more active role in its governance after the trials, ensuring that colonial leaders were more accountable to the Crown. This shift marked the beginning of a gradual decline in theocratic rule in New England and a move toward more balanced governance.

Thus, the Salem witch trials sent shockwaves through New England, influencing neighboring colonies and leaving a lasting legacy on governance and the region's reputation. While the immediate effects were felt most strongly in Massachusetts, the trials served as a powerful reminder to all the colonies of the dangers of religious extremism and unchecked fear. The echoes of Salem would continue to shape New England's social and political landscape for decades to come.

CHAPTER 6

The Trials: Justice or Travesty?

Legal Procedures in Colonial Massachusetts

In colonial Massachusetts, legal procedures were deeply rooted in English common law, but they also reflected the Puritan society's desire to maintain order and morality in line with their religious convictions. Standard legal processes followed a system that involved magistrates, judges, and juries, with trials that were generally expected to be fair, structured, and consistent with the law. However, when it came to the witch trials of 1692, many of these conventional procedures were set aside or significantly altered, leading to outcomes that would be considered unjust by modern standards.

Standard Legal Procedures in Colonial Massachusetts

There was no formal system of professional judges as we understand them today. Instead, magistrates played a dual role in both prosecuting and judging cases. In criminal trials, the accused were entitled to a jury of their peers, and trials usually followed a process of accusation, investigation, evidence presentation, and then deliberation by the jury.

One of the fundamental principles of colonial law was the right to a fair trial. Evidence, whether it be eyewitness testimony or physical proof, was essential for securing a conviction. The accused had the opportunity to confront their accusers, present their own defense, and call witnesses on their behalf. While the system was not perfect and was influenced by the religious and moral biases of the time, there was still a basic expectation that justice would be served based on the facts.

Legal Practices During the Witch Trials

The Salem witch trials, however, deviated sharply from these established norms. Between the winter of 1692 and the spring of 1693, a series of trials unfolded that resulted in the execution of 19 people and the imprisonment of many others, all accused of witchcraft. During this period, the usual legal safeguards were suspended, and the trials took on a character of mass hysteria and fear.

One of the most glaring differences was the way in which evidence was handled. In the Salem trials, spectral evidence—testimony that the spirit or specter of the accused had appeared to the witness in a dream or vision—was admissible in court. This type of evidence would never have been allowed in a standard colonial trial, as it was inherently subjective and impossible to corroborate. Nevertheless, spectral evidence became a cornerstone of many convictions. For example, during the trial of Bridget Bishop, one of the first to be convicted, witnesses claimed that her specter had tormented them in their sleep. Despite the lack of physical evidence or credible witnesses, Bishop was found guilty and executed.

Another significant departure from normal legal procedures was the manner in which confessions were obtained and valued. In colonial Massachusetts, a confession was generally viewed as a powerful piece of evidence but had to be voluntary and consistent with the facts of the case. In the witch trials, however, confessions were often obtained under duress or as a result of psychological pressure. Those who confessed to witchcraft were sometimes spared the death penalty, creating an incentive for the accused to make false confessions in the hope of saving their own lives. In some cases, individuals confessed to avoid further torture or to appease the court, which led to the proliferation of accusations as the confessors often implicated others.

The role of judges and magistrates also changed dramatically during the trials. Normally, judges were expected to remain impartial, ensuring that the trial adhered to the rule of law. However, during the witch trials, figures like Chief Magistrate William Stoughton took an active role in pushing for convictions. Stoughton, a devout Puritan and staunch believer in the existence of witches, often allowed questionable evidence, including spectral testimonies, and ignored pleas for reason or mercy. His aggressive pursuit of guilty verdicts set the tone for many of the trials, with disastrous consequences for the accused.

Juries, who typically would have deliberated on the evidence presented, were often swayed by the heightened emotions and the pressure exerted by the court and the broader community. The fear of witchcraft was so pervasive that jurors likely felt compelled to convict, even in cases where the evidence was flimsy or nonexistent. In the trial of Rebecca Nurse, a respected elderly woman, the jury initially returned a verdict of not guilty. However, under pressure from the judges and public outcry, the jury reconsidered and changed their verdict to guilty. Nurse was subsequently hanged, despite her long-standing reputation for piety and goodness.

Why Were Procedures Altered?

The modifications to standard legal procedures during the Salem witch trials can be attributed to several factors. First and foremost, the fear of witchcraft was deeply rooted in the religious worldview of the Puritan colonists. They believed that Satan was actively working in their midst, and the presence of witches was evidence of his influence. This belief made it easier for the court to accept evidence and procedures that would have been dismissed in other contexts. The urgency to root out evil, combined with a genuine belief that the colony's spiritual and physical safety was at stake, led to a suspension of rational legal principles.

Secondly, the social and political climate of the time contributed to the legal irregularities. The colony had recently experienced significant upheaval, including threats from Native American attacks, political instability, and economic challenges. In such a tense environment, the witch trials provided a means of channeling the community's anxieties into a single, seemingly manageable issue. The trials offered a scapegoat for the colony's troubles, and the rapid convictions helped restore a sense of control, even if it was based on misguided notions of justice.

Finally, personal rivalries and local disputes played a significant role in how the trials were conducted. Many of the accusations of witchcraft stemmed from longstanding grudges between families, neighbors, and factions within the community. In the case of Martha Corey, her outspoken criticism of the trials led to her own accusation and conviction, illustrating how personal animosities could influence the legal process.

Thus, the Salem witch trials represented a stark departure from the legal norms of colonial Massachusetts. The abandonment of standard procedures, the reliance on spectral evidence, and the manipulation of confessions and juries all contributed to a system of justice that was deeply flawed and driven by fear rather than reason. Figures like William Stoughton, who wielded enormous influence during the trials, played a key role in allowing these legal distortions to take place. The legacy of these trials serves as a cautionary tale about the dangers of abandoning legal principles in the face of mass hysteria, fear, and religious extremism.

The Role of Confessions

The role of confessions in the Salem witch trials cannot be overstated. At the heart of the trials was the widespread belief in the supernatural, fueled by fear, hysteria, and an ingrained sense of religious duty. For the Puritans of Salem, the very idea that some among them might have made a pact with the Devil threatened the community's spiritual fabric. In this climate, confessions became both a powerful tool for the prosecution and a desperate strategy for survival. Analyzing why some of the accused chose to confess, the consequences of these confessions, and the methods used to extract them offers a chilling insight into the machinery of fear that drove the witch hunt.

Why Some Accused Chose to Confess

One of the most perplexing aspects of the Salem witch trials is why some of the accused, even those with no evidence against them, chose to confess to crimes they had not committed. However, it's crucial to consider the psychological and social pressures they faced. In Puritan theology, confession was seen as the first step toward redemption. Confessing one's sins allowed for the possibility of forgiveness, not only from the community but from God. For many accused witches, particularly those who were already vulnerable—whether through poverty, social isolation, or previous brushes with the law—confession might have seemed like the only chance to avoid the gallows.

One such case is that of Tituba, the enslaved woman from the Caribbean who was among the first to be accused. Tituba's confession set the stage for the escalating rage. After being beaten and threatened by her master, Reverend Samuel Parris, she confessed to witchcraft, telling a tale of diabolical pacts, strange creatures, and flight through the night. Tituba's confession not only spared her life but also fanned the flames of suspicion and panic, as it seemed to confirm the community's worst fears about a pervasive satanic conspiracy. She named other witches, leading to a cascade of accusations and further confessions. In her case, the psychological and physical coercion was evident, and her confession became a means of self-preservation.

Another factor that influenced confessions was the simple, stark reality of what lay ahead for those who did not confess. Those who denied the accusations were far more likely to be executed than those who confessed.

The trials were a cruel paradox: those who admitted guilt were spared the death penalty and often imprisoned, while those who maintained their innocence were condemned to hang. Faced with such choices, many chose to confess as a way to survive, however temporarily.

Methods of Extracting Confessions

The confessions obtained during the Salem witch trials were not the result of calm, rational introspection. They were often extracted through intense psychological pressure and, in some cases, outright torture or physical coercion. The court and the community believed so firmly in the existence of witches that they were willing to employ extreme measures to root them out.

One of the most common methods of extracting confessions was relentless interrogation. Accused individuals were brought before magistrates and subjected to long hours of questioning, during which they were bombarded with leading questions, accusations, and threats. The interrogations were designed to break down the accused, creating an atmosphere of fear and confusion. The sheer intensity of the questioning often led to desperation and exhaustion, making it easier for individuals to confess to crimes they had not committed.

For example, in the case of Sarah Good, one of the earliest accused women, the questioning was brutal. Good, who was poor and already marginalized within the community, was repeatedly asked about her involvement with the Devil. She denied the accusations but was repeatedly badgered with the same questions. At one point, she was told that her four-year-old daughter had implicated her in witchcraft, a psychological blow that undoubtedly contributed to her mental breakdown. Though she did not confess, her mental state and poverty made her a convenient target, and her denial was treated with suspicion.

Physical coercion also played a role in extracting confessions. While the Salem trials did not use the same formalized torture methods employed in European witch hunts, the accused were often kept in appalling conditions that amounted to a form of physical and mental torture. They were shackled in chains, confined to tiny cells, and deprived of basic needs. In this environment, the prospect of confession became more appealing, as it often meant being spared from the physical torment of imprisonment.

The Reliability of Confessions

Despite the prevalence of confessions during the Salem witch trials, their reliability was highly questionable. The confessions were often contradictory, inconsistent, and clearly influenced by external pressures. In many cases, those who confessed quickly recanted their statements once the immediate threat of execution was lifted. This suggests that the confessions were not the result of genuine guilt but rather a response to the overwhelming fear and coercion that permeated the trials.

The case of Rebecca Nurse provides a striking example of the dubious nature of confessions. Nurse, a respected elderly woman, was initially found not guilty by the jury. However, the community's outrage at this verdict, coupled with pressure from the judges, led the jury to reconsider. Nurse never confessed, maintaining her innocence until her execution. Her refusal to confess, even under extreme pressure, was seen as evidence of her guilt in the eyes of the court. In contrast, those who did confess, like Sarah Churchill, were often seen as redeemable and were spared the death penalty, even though their confessions were rife with inconsistencies and seemed to be motivated by a desire to save themselves rather than a truthful admission of guilt.

The Consequences of Confessions

The consequences of confessions during the Salem witch trials were profound. For those who confessed, the immediate result was often a stay of execution, but their lives were forever altered. They were branded as witches, their reputations destroyed, and many spent months or even years in prison. Moreover, their confessions had a ripple effect, leading to further accusations and escalating the panic. Each confession seemed to confirm the existence of a vast conspiracy of witches, which in turn justified the continuation of the trials.

The confessions also had a lasting impact on the community. As the number of confessions grew, so too did the belief that Salem was under siege by a diabolical force. This belief created an atmosphere of paranoia, where even the most tenuous accusations were taken seriously. The confessions, though often coerced and unreliable, became the backbone of the trials, driving them forward and ensuring that more innocent people would be accused.

However, the confessions of the Salem witch trials reveal the deep psychological and social forces at work in this tragic chapter of American history. They were not merely admissions of guilt but the product of a system designed to break individuals down, to strip them of their dignity, and to force them into compliance with a narrative of fear and superstition. The Salem witch trials stand as a cautionary tale of what can happen when reason is overwhelmed by hysteria, and when confessions, no matter how unreliable, are used as tools of persecution.

Giles Corey: Pressed to Death

Giles Corey, a wealthy, 81-year-old farmer from Salem Village, was an unlikely figure to become one of the most harrowing symbols of the Salem Witch Trials. His death by pressing — a brutal and rare form of torture — would forever mark his legacy and distinguish him from the dozens of others accused of witchcraft. What led him to endure such an agonizing fate, his body crushed beneath the relentless weight of stones, rather than enter a plea? The story of Giles Corey is both a fascinating narrative of personal resolve and an impressive reflection on the legal and moral injustices of the Salem witch trials.

Refusal to Plead: The Beginning of the End

In April 1692, Giles Corey was accused of witchcraft. His own wife, Martha Corey, had already been accused and arrested, having spoken out against the trials. Corey's own involvement in the proceedings was complex. Initially, he had supported the witch hunt, even testifying against his wife. But soon, the relentless anxieties would envelop him as well. Accused by several local girls, including Ann Putnam, who claimed that Corey's specter had appeared to them and tormented them, the elderly farmer was arrested and brought to trial.

When asked to plead *"guilty"* or *"not guilty"* to the charges of witchcraft, Giles Corey remained silent. This refusal to enter a plea was highly unusual. In English common law, upon which colonial legal practices were based, a defendant's silence in the face of such a charge prevented the court from proceeding to trial. Without a plea, there could be no trial, and without a trial, no formal conviction.

But Corey's refusal came with severe consequences. Colonial law permitted the use of "peine forte et dure"

(French for "strong and hard punishment") for those who refused to enter a plea. The intent was to force a confession or plea by torturing the accused — in Corey's case, through the ancient and rare method of pressing.

The Pressing: A Slow, Agonizing Death

On September 19, 1692, Corey was subjected to pressing in a field near Salem's jail. The process of pressing was excruciatingly simple and horribly effective. Giles Corey was stripped down and laid on his back in a pit. A large board, or door, was placed on top of him. Then, heavy stones were slowly placed on the board, one by one, each adding more unbearable weight. The intention was to induce the accused to speak as the pressure built on their chest, crushing their ribs, making it harder to breathe.

Sensory details from this torturous process paint a harrowing picture. Imagine the oppressive sound of each stone as it was added, a dull thud followed by a crunch as Corey's bones creaked under the weight. The hot September air thick with dust and the smell of sweat and earth would have surrounded him. His breath, at first steady but growing more labored, would have become shallow, wheezing gasps as the minutes dragged into hours. His eyes might have rolled back into his head as the pain grew unbearable, but he said nothing. Witnesses reported that each time Corey was asked to enter a plea, he responded only with "More weight." His tongue, crushed beneath the ever-increasing weight, had to be forced back into his mouth.

The pressing continued for two agonizing days. Each hour must have felt like an eternity for Corey, with death approaching slowly but inevitably. The weight of the stones increased gradually, and with it, the pain. The bones of his ribcage strained and eventually began to snap. His chest collapsed under the pressure, squeezing the life out of him inch by inch. The silence around him must have been as unbearable as the pain, broken only by the occasional grunt of exertion from the men placing the stones. Finally, on the second day, Giles Corey died. He had never entered a plea.

Corey's Motivation: Why Stay Silent?

Why did Giles Corey refuse to plead? His silence was both an act of defiance and a calculated decision. If Corey had pleaded guilty, he would have likely faced execution by hanging, the same fate as many others convicted during the trials. However, if he had pleaded not guilty and still been found guilty — a near certainty given the hysteria of the times — his estate would have been forfeited to the government. By refusing to enter a plea, Corey ensured that his property would pass to his heirs upon his death, rather than being seized by the authorities.

Yet there may have been more at work than just protecting his estate. Some historians suggest that Corey's silence was also an act of resistance against the witch trials themselves. By refusing to cooperate, he denied the court the satisfaction of a formal trial and conviction. In a sense, he was protesting the very system that had ensnared him. His final words, *"More weight,"* have been interpreted as a symbol of his defiance — a man unwilling to yield to the absurd and unjust proceedings of the Salem witch trials, even under the most extreme torture.

Legal and Moral Implications

The death of Giles Corey holds a unique place in the history of the Salem witch trials. Legally, his case was a stark reminder of the brutality of colonial justice and the dangerous power of unchecked authority. The practice of pressing had long been abandoned in England, and even in the colonies, it was rare. Corey's pressing to death was the only recorded instance in American history.

The moral implications of Corey's ordeal are equally profound. His death by pressing represents the inhuman lengths to which the Salem authorities were willing to go to enforce their version of justice. Corey's refusal to plead — and the court's willingness to torture him for it — exposes the fragile line between law and cruelty during the witch trials. It also raises questions about the ethical responsibilities of those in power.

Legacy of Giles Corey

The legacy of Giles Corey resonates powerfully today. His refusal to yield under extreme duress has made him a symbol of resistance. While other accused witches were victims of unjust trials, Corey's fate stands out as a man who chose to face death rather than bend to the will of a broken system. His silence was, in its own way, a powerful voice against the chaos and irrationality of the witch trials.

In the centuries since his death, Corey has become a tragic yet heroic figure in the narrative of the Salem witch trials. His story reminds us of the dangers of mob mentality, the perils of unchecked power, and the human capacity for both cruelty and courage. The stones that crushed his body symbolized the weight of fear and superstition that crushed Salem in 1692. And in the end, it was Giles Corey's silence that spoke the loudest.

CHAPTER 7

Gender, Power, and Persecution

Women as Witches: Stereotypes and Reality

The Salem Witch Trials of 1692 were deeply rooted in the gender dynamics of colonial New England, where societal expectations and stereotypes about women played a central role in who was accused and how they were treated. The majority of the accused were women, and this was not a coincidence. Witchcraft, a crime long associated with women, stemmed from the belief that women were inherently more susceptible to evil and temptation. These accusations were a reflection of deep-seated misogyny that is prejudice against women and girls, where the prevailing stereotypes about women shaped who was targeted during the rampage and how they were prosecuted.

Stereotypes of Witches and Women

In 17th-century New England, society held rigid beliefs about gender roles. Women were expected to be submissive, pious, and subservient to men. They were relegated to domestic roles, managing households, raising children, and adhering to strict Puritan values. Women who deviated from these norms were viewed with suspicion. Independent, outspoken, or non-conforming women were often labeled as troublesome or dangerous, and this stigma often translated into witchcraft accusations.

The stereotype of the "witch" in Salem and beyond was often tied to these gendered perceptions. Witches were thought to be older women, widows, or those without male protection or financial independence. They were frequently depicted as embittered, antisocial, and manipulative, possessing the power to harm others through curses, spells, or consorting with the devil. This belief reflected broader societal fears about women's potential to disrupt the established patriarchal order.

Moreover, women were seen as more spiritually vulnerable than men. This notion can be traced back to religious teachings that emphasized Eve's role in original sin, framing women as inherently more prone to moral weakness. In the Puritan mindset, this made women more likely to be seduced by Satan. Women were often accused of witchcraft based on their alleged relationships with the devil, reinforcing the idea that they were naturally inclined towards evil. For example, one of the earliest accused, Tituba, a slave woman, was not only a victim of racism but also of the prevailing gendered assumptions about witches.

Gender Dynamics of Accusations

In the context of the Salem witch hunt, the gender dynamics were starkly evident. Women, especially those who were independent, outspoken, or deviated from traditional roles, became prime targets for accusations. The Puritanical society of New England adhered to rigid gender norms, where women were expected to be submissive, nurturing, and obedient. Those who challenged these expectations—whether through behavior, social status, or property ownership—were often viewed with suspicion.

The majority of the accused were women, with estimates suggesting that around 78% of the individuals charged with witchcraft were female. This ratio not only underscores the gendered nature of the accusations but also reflects the pervasive stereotypes that labeled women as more susceptible to temptation and evil. The notion of women as inherently weaker and more prone to moral failings was deeply rooted in Puritan theology and societal beliefs.

Treatment of Accused Women

The treatment of women accused of witchcraft during the Salem trials starkly contrasted with historical norms regarding punishment and justice. Accused witches faced trials that were heavily biased against them, often lacking fundamental legal protections. Spectral evidence, which allowed witnesses to testify about visions or apparitions of the accused, was widely accepted, creating an environment where mere accusation could lead to conviction. One notable case is that of Rebecca Nurse, a respected member of the community who was accused of witchcraft at the age of 71.

In contrast, men accused of witchcraft often experienced a different fate. While there were some male defendants, they were fewer in number, and many received more leniency in their trials. For example, George Burroughs, a former minister, was hanged, but he was an exception rather than the rule. The overwhelming majority of those executed were women, further demonstrating the gender disparity in accusations and outcomes.

Statistical Overview

The statistics surrounding the Salem witch trials reveal a troubling pattern of gender disparity. Of the 200 individuals accused, approximately 141 were women, and 19 of these women were executed. In contrast, only four men were executed, and several others were imprisoned but not sentenced to death. This stark difference points to a systemic bias that favored the prosecution of women, highlighting the intersection of gender and power dynamics in colonial society.

Additionally, the age of the accused played a significant role in the trials. Many of the women targeted were older, often widowed or single, which placed them outside the traditional family structure that offered protection. The fear of these independent women taking on roles that challenged patriarchal authority fueled accusations and societal hysteria.

Legacy of Gendered Accusations

The legacy of the Salem witch trials continues to resonate in discussions about gender and power dynamics today. The trials serve as a cautionary tale about the dangers of scapegoating and the consequences of societal fears directed toward women who do not conform to established norms. The stereotypes surrounding witches not only influenced the trials but also laid the groundwork for ongoing societal attitudes toward women who defy convention.

After a thorough check of the Salem witch trials, it becomes clear that the accusations were not merely about witchcraft; they were deeply intertwined with the gendered nature of colonial society. The stereotypes and realities faced by women during this tumultuous period, were ones in which fear, power, and gender intersected to shape one of the most infamous aspects in American history.

However, the Salem witch trials reveals how societal fears can manifest in destructive ways, particularly against marginalized groups. The overwhelming number of women accused and convicted during this period reflects enduring stereotypes and the harsh realities of life for those who dared to challenge the status quo.

Property and Inheritance: Hidden Motives

Property and inheritance played a pivotal role in the Salem witch trials, influencing several accusations and shaping the dynamics of these tragic events. Beneath the religious fervor and the fear of witchcraft lay hidden motives tied to land disputes, economic ambition, and the precarious legal status of women in colonial Massachusetts. Many of the accused, often women, were targets due to their ties to property or inheritance, making the trials not only a reflection of societal fear but also an avenue for opportunistic individuals seeking financial gain or control over valuable assets.

Economic Factors Behind Witchcraft Accusations

At the heart of the Salem witch trials were economic tensions. Colonial Massachusetts was a community deeply reliant on land for wealth and survival. Land ownership was a crucial aspect of social standing and prosperity, and disputes over property could easily escalate into personal conflicts. In some cases, these conflicts found expression in accusations of witchcraft.

An example of this is the study of George Burroughs, a former minister of Salem Village who became embroiled in disputes over unpaid debts. Burroughs was accused of witchcraft and executed in 1692, partly due to lingering animosity regarding property. His financial struggles had left him in conflict with members of the community, who may have used the witch trials as an opportunity to settle old scores. While religious concerns certainly played a role in his downfall, his economic misfortunes undoubtedly contributed to his vulnerability.

Similarly, the case of Bridget Bishop highlights how property could be a hidden factor in accusations. Bishop, a well-known tavern owner, was an independent woman who owned property in her own right, which was unusual for the time. Her independence and defiance of societal norms made her a target. Accusers may have viewed her economic autonomy as a threat, and her property holdings could have provided additional motivation for her prosecution. Bishop's ownership of land and her refusal to conform to expected female behavior likely heightened the suspicion against her, resulting in her execution.

The Legal Status of Women in Colonial Massachusetts

Women in colonial Massachusetts were particularly vulnerable to witchcraft accusations due to their legal status. Legally, women were often dependent on male relatives—fathers, husbands, or brothers—for financial security and protection. They were generally not allowed to own property in their own names unless they were widows. Even then, their hold on property was tenuous, as male relatives or creditors could contest their ownership.

Widows, especially those without male heirs, were in a precarious position, and many of the women accused of witchcraft fit this profile. When a woman inherited land or property, it often aroused suspicion, envy, or outright hostility from others in the community, particularly if there were competing claims to the inheritance. In some cases, these tensions over property would manifest as accusations of witchcraft.

For instance, Sarah Good, one of the first women accused during the trials, was a destitute woman whose land had been lost due to her husband's mismanagement. Her poverty and bitterness towards her neighbors made her an easy target, as she was seen as a disruptive figure in the community. Although she did not own land, her case illustrates how economic desperation could lead to social ostracism, making individuals like her prime candidates for witchcraft accusations.

Inheritance Disputes and Witchcraft Accusations

Inheritance disputes were another significant factor driving witchcraft accusations. When land or wealth passed from one generation to the next, it often sparked conflict among family members or with neighbors. In a patriarchal society where women had limited rights to property, any suggestion that a woman might gain control over an estate could be viewed with suspicion and resentment. Witchcraft accusations, in such cases, were a way to undermine a woman's claim to property.

The case of Susannah Martin is illustrative of this. Martin, a widow from Amesbury, had been involved in numerous legal battles over property, particularly concerning her inheritance from her father. Her attempts to secure what she believed was rightfully hers led to a long-standing feud with several neighbors, which culminated in her being accused of witchcraft. Martin's assertiveness in legal matters, coupled with her disputes over land, made her an easy target for accusations. She was ultimately convicted and executed, highlighting how property disputes could fuel witchcraft allegations.

Similarly, the case of Elizabeth Proctor reveals the intersection of inheritance and witchcraft accusations.

Proctor's husband, John, was a wealthy farmer, and the Proctors owned a considerable amount of land. Elizabeth's connection to this wealth made her a target, as others in the community may have sought to weaken the Proctors' standing by accusing her of witchcraft. Both Elizabeth and her husband were accused, and while John was executed, Elizabeth's pregnancy spared her life for a time. Their case underscores how economic envy and inheritance concerns could play a role in the witch trials.

Broader Economic Context

The broader economic context of colonial Massachusetts also helps explain why property and inheritance played such a crucial role in the witch trials. By the late 17th century, the region was experiencing significant economic changes. The population was growing, putting increased pressure on available land, which had become the primary source of wealth. This scarcity of land led to heightened competition and conflict among settlers, particularly in communities like Salem Village, where agricultural land was essential for survival.

In this environment of economic tension, accusations of witchcraft could serve as a tool to remove rivals or settle disputes over land. Accusing someone of witchcraft not only damaged their reputation but could also result in their execution, leaving their property available for others to claim. This was especially true for women who inherited land, as their control over property was often seen as illegitimate or temporary in the eyes of male relatives or neighbors.

Thus, Property disputes and inheritance played an undeniable role in fueling the Salem witch trials, revealing the complex interplay of economic motives, gender dynamics, and legal structures. Women's vulnerable legal status in colonial Massachusetts made them particularly susceptible to accusations, as their ownership of property or involvement in inheritance disputes aroused suspicion and envy. In many cases, hidden motives tied to land and wealth were just as significant as religious or supernatural fears in driving the accusations. Through cases like those of George Burroughs, Bridget Bishop, and Susannah Martin, it becomes clear that the Salem witch trials were not only a product of mass hysteria but also a reflection of deeper economic conflicts and power struggles within the community.

Men Accused: Breaking the Pattern

In Salem witch trials, the overwhelming focus tends to fall on women accused of witchcraft. However, men also found themselves entangled in the agitation,, though their experiences often diverged from those of women.

The Trials and Convictions of Men

One of the most notable differences is the sheer number of accusations. Of the 200 individuals accused of witchcraft in Salem, fewer than 30 were men. This discrepancy can be attributed to the gendered nature of witchcraft as it was perceived during the period. Women, especially those who were older, widowed, or otherwise marginalized, were more likely to be seen as embodying traits associated with witchcraft, such as defiance of social norms or independence from male authority. Men, by contrast, were not as easily associated with these transgressions. Moreover, societal structures positioned men in roles of power, making them less likely to be scapegoated during moments of panic.

Although fewer men were accused, their trials followed a similar process to those of women, with charges based on spectral evidence, confessions extracted under duress, and testimonies from accusers claiming to have seen their spirits performing malicious deeds. However, men generally had more social capital and could draw on their status and networks to defend themselves more effectively than women. Some men, like John Proctor, actively fought back against the absurdity of the trials, questioning the validity of the evidence presented against them. Nonetheless, resistance often proved futile, and men like Proctor were executed despite their protests.

However, fewer men were executed compared to women. Of the 20 executed during the trials, five were men. The lower number of male executions may be partly due to the perception that women were more susceptible to the Devil's influence and therefore more likely to engage in witchcraft.

Profiles of Accused Men

Several men stand out in the annals of the Salem witch trials, revealing the differences in how gender influenced their accusations and trials:

Samuel Wardwell

Samuel Wardwell was a carpenter and fortune-teller who had previously dabbled in palm reading and telling fortunes. Unlike many accused men, Wardwell confessed to making a pact with the Devil under intense pressure and threats during his trial. However, after retracting his confession and claiming his innocence, he was convicted and hanged in September 1692. His background in fortune-telling, typically seen as a suspicious occupation associated with women, made him a target for accusations.

Wardwell's case shows that men involved in traditionally "magical" or superstitious activities could also be accused, though their confessions and social status did not always protect them from execution. His fortune-telling may have contributed to his being seen as straddling the line between acceptable behavior for men and the transgressive activities typically associated with witchcraft.

Roger Toothaker

Roger Toothaker was a farmer and folk healer who practiced "counter-magic" and claimed to have special knowledge of how to combat witches. His practices of folk healing and counter-witchcraft brought him under suspicion. He was accused of witchcraft by the afflicted girls in Salem, and his arrest followed. Unlike many other accused men, Toothaker died in jail before he could be tried or executed, succumbing to illness in June 1692.

His case reveals how men who engaged in alternative healing practices—another domain usually associated with women—could also become suspects during the trials. Toothaker's work in combating witchcraft ironically made him a target, illustrating how any association with magic, even benevolent or protective magic, could be dangerous.

Philip English

Philip English was a successful and wealthy merchant from Salem, originally from the Channel Islands. English's affluence and prominence in the community made him a target of the witchcraft accusations, particularly because of his strained relationships with some of the Puritan leadership in Salem. Accused alongside his wife, Mary English, Philip managed to escape imprisonment and fled to New York before he could be tried. He later returned to Salem after the hysteria subsided and successfully reclaimed his property.

English's case unviels how wealth and social connections could provide a way to evade trial, especially for men.

While many women lacked the resources or networks to escape imprisonment, English's status allowed him to avoid conviction, showing a significant difference in how men of means could navigate the accusations.

William Barker Sr

William Barker Sr., an elderly man from Andover, confessed to making a pact with the Devil and implicated others in his confession. He claimed that the Devil promised him wealth and freedom from his debts, a temptation Barker may have succumbed to due to his poverty. Barker's confession under duress led to further accusations against others, including his own son, William Barker Jr., and his daughter, Mary Barker. Unlike many of the other accused men, Barker's confession did not spare him from conviction, but he was not executed, possibly because of his age or the shifting tides of the trials.

Barker's case is significant because it shows how men from lower economic standings could be swept into the hysteria, often through coerced confessions. His age and financial struggles made him vulnerable, though the trials primarily targeted women in similar circumstances.

John Alden Jr

John Alden Jr., the son of Mayflower settlers and a prominent member of the Boston community, was accused of witchcraft during the trials. Alden was a sea captain and trader, and his interactions with the afflicted girls in Salem during his time in the area led to his accusation. He was arrested but managed to escape from jail in Boston before his trial and fled to New York. Like Philip English, Alden was able to use his wealth, status, and connections to avoid conviction, and he was later exonerated when the trials ended.

Alden's case demonstrates how prominent men could be caught up in the witchcraft hysteria, but their social position often afforded them opportunities to escape punishment. His successful evasion of the trials stands in contrast to the fates of many women, who were more likely to lack the resources to flee or mount a defense.

Gender and the Accusation Process

The gender dynamics at play in Salem reveal much about the broader societal roles of men and women. While women were seen as more inherently vulnerable to sin and the Devil's influence due to their perceived moral weakness, men were often associated with leadership and authority. This likely explains why accusations against men were less common and often involved more prominent figures. The men who were accused were often perceived as threats to the social order in ways that differed from women—through challenges to religious or political authority, for instance, rather than through the subversion of traditional gender roles.

While both men and women faced the terror of the Salem witch trials, gender significantly shaped their experiences. Fewer men were accused, and their social status often allowed them to mount more robust defenses.

CHAPTER 8

The Beginning of the End

Growing Doubts and Opposition

The Salem witch trials, once fervently supported by a community in the grip of hysteria, soon began to face a growing wave of doubt and opposition. As the number of accusations spread and the methods of determining guilt grew increasingly dubious, cracks started to appear in the fervor surrounding the trials. Colonists and officials alike began to question the legitimacy of the proceedings, sowing seeds of doubt that would eventually contribute to their end.

One of the earliest and most prominent critics of the trials was Thomas Brattle, a well-respected Boston merchant and intellectual. Brattle's opposition came at a time when many were still swept up in the fear of witchcraft, but his letter, written in October 1692, stands as one of the most reasoned and articulate condemnations of the proceedings. Brattle condemned the use of "spectral evidence," the primary method by which the accused were convicted. Spectral evidence, which consisted of the afflicted claiming that the specter or spirit of the accused had attacked them, was nearly impossible to disprove and required no tangible proof. In

Brattle's view, the reliance on such evidence was an affront to reason and justice. He wrote:

"I cannot but condemn, and lament the countenance that hath been given by many to these things, whereby multitudes of innocent persons have been accused, condemned, and executed."

Brattle's letter represents a critical turning point. He directly challenged the credibility of the afflicted girls whose accusations were at the heart of the trials. Brattle questioned how it was possible for these girls to claim they could see spirits while others could not. His skepticism extended to the larger theological issues at play, noting that the belief in spectral evidence was a dangerous departure from the legal standards that should have governed the colony. Brattle's arguments resonated with many who had previously remained silent, as the absurdity of the accusations became harder to ignore.

Other figures also began to speak out, though they often did so in more cautious tones. The Reverend Increase Mather, father of the more infamous Cotton Mather, became another voice of reason during the trials. While Increase Mather had initially supported the efforts to root out witches, his position changed as the trials dragged on and more people were accused. In his work Cases of Conscience Concerning Evil Spirits, published in late 1692, Mather expressed grave concerns about the reliance on spectral evidence. His famous line, *"It were better that ten suspected witches should escape than that one innocent person should be condemned,"* captured the growing unease among many colonists.

Mather's argument represented a shift from the initial impulse to purge the community of witches at all costs. He, like Brattle, understood that the use of questionable evidence could lead to the condemnation of innocent people. Mather's words also had a theological weight, given his stature in the community as a prominent Puritan minister. He warned that the devil could just as easily use the courts to condemn the innocent as he could use witches to harm the godly.

The shifting tide of public opinion was also fueled by the sheer number of accusations that were being made. By mid-1692, the courts were overwhelmed with cases, and the accusations had spread far beyond Salem to neighboring communities. Families that had once been respected members of the community now found themselves embroiled in the witchcraft hysteria. For many colonists, the realization that the trials could affect anyone—regardless of their standing in society—brought a new sense of urgency to the growing opposition. No longer was it just the outcasts or the poor being accused; now, prominent figures like John Proctor and Rebecca Nurse were standing trial.

In addition to the voices of prominent men, women also played a critical role in shaping opposition to the trials. While their influence may not have been as widely documented, it was often in the private sphere, within families and communities, that doubts about the legitimacy of the trials first arose. The testimony of individuals like Mary Easty, who maintained her innocence to the very end, moved many to question the integrity of the process. Easty's poignant petition to the court, just days before her execution, begged that no more innocent blood be shed, as she knew herself to be innocent. Her calm demeanor in the face of death stood in stark contrast to the difficulties surrounding the trials and left a lasting impression on those who witnessed it.

Public opinion shifted further as more people became aware of the flaws in the judicial process. Magistrates who had once been staunch supporters of the trials began to waver. Samuel Sewall, a judge during the trials, would later publicly repent for his role in the convictions. His famous Day of Humiliation in 1697, where he stood before the congregation of the Old South Church in Boston and confessed his guilt, was a powerful symbol of the growing recognition that the trials had been a miscarriage of justice.

The turning point came when Governor William Phips intervened in October 1692. Phips, who had initially supported the trials, grew increasingly concerned as the accusations escalated and even reached the family of his wife. He suspended the Court of Oyer and Terminer, which had been responsible for the executions, and later ordered that spectral evidence should no longer be considered in the trials. In doing so, Phips effectively ended the most violent phase of the witch hunt, and by the spring of 1693, the remaining accused were either acquitted or released.

However, the arguments put forth by critics like Thomas Brattle and Increase Mather, along with the shift in public opinion, played a crucial role in bringing an end to the trials. Their insistence on reason, legal standards, and the dangers of relying on spectral evidence helped to expose the flaws in the process and ultimately saved many lives. The Salem witch trials, which had begun with such fervor, were now seen as a dark chapter in the history of Colonial Massachusetts—a cautionary tale about the dangers of mass hysteria and the importance of justice tempered by reason.

The legacy of those who opposed the trials endures as a testament to the power of doubt and critical thinking in the face of overwhelming fear. Their voices remind us that even in times of hysteria, there are always those who are willing to stand against the tide, guided by principles of fairness and justice.

Governor Phips' Intervention

Governor William Phips' role in the Salem witch trials marked one of the most critical turning points in the turbulent saga. His intervention, though late, brought a semblance of order to a legal process that had spiraled into chaos. Phips himself had initially supported the trials, but as events unfolded, pressure mounted, and the realization of the miscarriage of justice became unavoidable. The journey from his early endorsement to his eventual intervention is one of political, religious, and personal awakening.

In 1692, William Phips was not merely a governor trying to manage the trials. He was a man newly installed in power, a figure navigating the treacherous political waters of a colony rife with fear, religious fervor, and factionalism. When the accusations of witchcraft began, Phips was away in Maine on a military campaign, fighting against the French and their Native American allies. By the time he returned to Massachusetts in May, the witchcraft hysteria was well underway, and in his absence, chaos had taken root in the colony.

Phips, largely unfamiliar with the details of what was unfolding, deferred to those he trusted. One of those was his trusted advisor and longtime friend, Increase Mather, as well as the influential Cotton Mather, Increase's son. Another was the man he appointed as Chief Justice of the special court overseeing the trials, William Stoughton. Stoughton, along with a panel of judges, took a hardline approach in prosecuting the accused, relying heavily on spectral evidence—the dubious testimony that alleged witches had sent their spirits to harm others.

At first, Phips did little to intervene. He was swept up in the widespread belief that the colony was under siege by dark forces, and like many of his contemporaries, he viewed the trials as necessary to protect Massachusetts from demonic threats. However, cracks in his confidence began to show as more and more people, including members of respected families, were accused. By September 1692, when several high-profile executions had already taken place, the tide of public opinion began to shift. The executions of figures like Bridget Bishop, John Proctor, and Martha Corey brought the weight of the tragedy into sharp relief.

Phips was also receiving letters from across the colony, from citizens deeply concerned about the legitimacy of the trials. Even some of the clergy, who had initially supported the proceedings, were now beginning to express their doubts. Notably, Increase Mather published a treatise in the fall of 1692, Cases of Conscience Concerning Evil Spirits, where he argued against the reliance on spectral evidence, stating that it was better to let a guilty person go free than to condemn an innocent person.

In response to the growing criticism and the evident flaws in the judicial process, Phips took decisive action. On October 29, 1692, he dissolved the Court of Oyer and Terminer, the tribunal that had been created specifically to deal with the witch trials. The court had already sentenced nineteen people to death, and many more had been jailed. By shutting down this court, Phips halted the most notorious phase of the trials. In its place, he established a Superior Court of Judicature, which took a more cautious approach, no longer accepting spectral evidence as valid.

This decision did not come without significant personal and political risk. Phips faced criticism from hardline Puritans who believed that he was abandoning the colony's defense against witchcraft. His decision to intervene and change the course of the trials alienated some of his closest allies, including William Stoughton, who would later criticize Phips for caving to public pressure.

Yet Phips had likely been influenced not only by the protests of influential men like Increase Mather but also by his personal connection to the trials. In a remarkable turn of events, his own wife, Lady Mary Phips, was accused of witchcraft. Though the accusations never gained the traction of other cases, it may have been the final straw that pushed Phips toward action. The prospect of the hysteria reaching into his own household made the dangers of the unchecked trials all too real.

With the disbanding of the Court of Oyer and Terminer, the intensity of the trials began to wane. The new court, presided over by more moderate judges, ultimately acquitted most of the remaining prisoners. Although a few more people were condemned, no more executions took place after September 1692. Those imprisoned on witchcraft charges were eventually pardoned, and many of the convictions were overturned.

Governor Phips' intervention marked the beginning of the end for the Salem witch trials. His actions shifted the legal and moral framework that had allowed the hysteria to thrive. What had begun as a widespread panic, fueled by fear and religious fervor, was now subject to more sober scrutiny. The change in legal proceedings, the rejection of spectral evidence, and the release of prisoners all signaled a turning point. It became increasingly clear that the trials had not been about rooting out genuine threats, but rather the result of mass hysteria, compounded by personal vendettas, economic tensions, and deep-seated social divisions.

As the trials came to an end, Phips faced the task of managing the aftermath. He ordered that the public fast to seek atonement for the injustice that had been committed, hoping to heal the wounds that had torn the colony apart. But while his intervention was crucial in stopping the legal proceedings, the scars of the witch trials remained. Families had been shattered, reputations ruined, and the specter of witchcraft continued to haunt the region for years to come.

In the years following the trials, Phips' reputation remained relatively intact, though not without its blemishes. While some praised him for stepping in and curbing the witchcraft hysteria, others blamed him for allowing the trials to escalate in the first place. William Stoughton, in particular, never forgave Phips for undermining the work of the court. Nevertheless, Phips' decision to intervene was a turning point in the Salem witch trials, representing a moment where reason began to prevail over fear.

Ultimately, Phips' role in the trials illustrates the complexities of leadership during times of crisis. His initial passivity, born of trust in his appointed officials, gave way to action only when the cost of inaction became too high. In doing so, he helped bring an end to one of the darkest chapters in colonial American history, a chapter that would serve as a lasting reminder of the dangers of mass hysteria and unchecked judicial power.

The Last Executions

As the Salem witch trials neared their tragic conclusion, a heavy gloom settled over the town. It was late September 1692, and although the feverish accusations had slowed, the courts were still grinding on, ensnaring the lives of a few more unfortunate souls. Among them were eight men and women who would become the final victims of the agitation. Their names would be etched into the dark history of the trials, and their executions would mark the end of one of the most tragic episodes in colonial Massachusetts.

Martha Corey, Mary Easty, Samuel Wardwell, Mary Parker, Alice Parker, Ann Pudeator, Wilmot Redd, and Margaret Scott were among the last to be condemned. Some had stood accused for months, while others were relatively new victims. Each had faced the same harrowing process: the terror of arrest, the indignity of a trial that seemed predetermined, and the weight of false accusations that turned friends and neighbors against them. But by September, the atmosphere had begun to shift. Doubts were creeping into the minds of more and more people. Yet for these eight, it was too late.

The mood in Salem was different during these final executions compared to earlier ones. By now, many townsfolk had begun to question the validity of the trials. The sweeping accusations that had once seemed righteous now felt like a cruel madness. Reverend Increase Mather, one of the most influential Puritan ministers, had publicly condemned the use of spectral evidence—the claims that witches' spirits were tormenting their victims. His son, Cotton Mather, although still a believer in the existence of witches, had begun to step back from the more outrageous claims. The fervor that had gripped Salem throughout the summer of 1692 was fading, but not fast enough to save the lives of the final eight.

Martha Corey had always been a woman of strong convictions, and that strength may have contributed to her downfall. Early in the trials, she had openly criticized the proceedings, even suggesting that the afflicted girls were lying. Her defiance made her a target, and soon enough, she found herself in the same position as those she had defended. Despite maintaining her innocence until the end, her fate was sealed, and she stood on the gallows in September, her unwavering spirit unbroken even in the face of death.

Mary Easty, the sister of Rebecca Nurse, was another victim of the trials' final sweep. Like her sister, she was known as a pious, upstanding woman, and like her sister, she was accused of witchcraft. Easty's case was especially heartbreaking because she had been released from jail at one point after petitioning for her freedom, only to be re-arrested days later. Her calm dignity in the face of injustice made her a figure of sympathy for many in the town, but sympathy was not enough to save her. She was hanged on September 22, 1692, alongside the others.

The story of Samuel Wardwell illustrates the dangers of desperation in the face of relentless accusations. Wardwell, a carpenter by trade, initially confessed to witchcraft, hoping that a confession might spare his life as it had for others. But when he later recanted, denying that he had ever practiced witchcraft, the court saw this as a sign of deceit. In Salem, to confess and then retract was worse than maintaining innocence all along. His fate was sealed, and he, too, climbed the gallows steps in September.

As the day of the final executions approached, the mood in Salem grew tense. There was a palpable sense that these deaths might be the last—a final, irreversible act in a saga that had spiraled out of control. Yet there was also a growing realization that these executions, like those before them, were founded on flimsy evidence and mass hysteria. The weight of what had transpired over the past months seemed to settle on the town like a suffocating fog. People whispered of the injustice that had been done, but they whispered too late.

The execution site, a barren patch of land known as Proctor's Ledge, had become a place of grim ritual. On September 22, 1692, the final group of people condemned during the Salem Witch Trials were led to the gallows to be hanged. The gallows, a simple wooden structure that had been used for months during the trials, stood out sharply against the cloudy sky. The air was cool, and the crowd that gathered to watch seemed smaller than it had been for earlier executions. Maybe people were tired of watching these hangings, or perhaps they were starting to feel guilty about what had been happening and were afraid that being there might make them seem guilty too.

One by one, the condemned were hanged. The silence that followed each drop of the rope was heavier than any words. These were not strangers, after all—they were neighbors, fellow churchgoers, parents, and spouses. For many in the crowd, the reality of what had happened was beginning to set in. The sense of righteous indignation that had once fueled the trials had all but vanished, replaced by a somber recognition of the tragedy that had unfolded.

These final executions differed from earlier ones not only in the atmosphere surrounding them but also in the growing cracks in the legal foundation of the trials. Spectral evidence, once the cornerstone of the prosecutions, was increasingly seen as dubious. The afflicted girls, whose testimonies had sent so many to their deaths, were now viewed with skepticism. And as prominent figures in the colony began to speak out against the trials, it became clear that the tide was turning. But for Martha Corey, Mary Easty, Samuel Wardwell, and the others, this change came too late.

The deaths of these eight marked the end of the executions, but not the end of the witch trials themselves. In the weeks that followed, more accused witches remained in jail, awaiting trial or release. But the fervor had broken. Governor Phips, responding to the growing unease, eventually dissolved the special court that had overseen the trials and barred further use of spectral evidence.

The final executions of the Salem witch trials seem to encapsulate the senselessness and cruelty of the entire affair. These eight men and women, like those before them, were caught in a web of fear and superstition that had spiraled beyond reason. Their deaths were not just the end of their lives but the end of an era in which paranoia had overruled justice. And as the nooses tightened around their necks, Salem itself began to awaken from its fevered dream, only to face the harsh reality of what had been done in the name of righteousness.

CHAPTER 9

Aftermath and Reflection

Reversing Attainders and Compensations

After the terror of the Salem witch trials began to wane, the question of justice loomed heavily over Massachusetts. The courts had sentenced 19 people to hang, one man was crushed to death, and countless others were imprisoned or accused. While public opinion began to turn against the trials as early as 1693, it wasn't until the early 18th century that serious attempts were made to reverse the attainders of those convicted and offer some semblance of compensation to their families. This legal process, though intended to right the wrongs of the past, was fraught with complexities and uneven results.

Reversing an attainder was no simple act in colonial Massachusetts. An attainder was a formal legal declaration that stripped a person of their civil rights due to a conviction of treason or a felony—in this case, witchcraft. It meant that not only was the accused punished, but their family could be barred from inheriting their property, and their name remained tarnished in the public record. The legal machinery to reverse these judgments had to be carefully set in motion.

In the early 1700s, mounting public pressure and the vocal appeals of families and ministers like Samuel Sewall, a judge during the trials, led the Massachusetts General Court to take action. In 1709, a formal petition for redress was submitted to the General Court on behalf of several families who had lost relatives in the trials. Among them were the relatives of John Proctor, Rebecca Nurse, and others who had been wrongly executed. These families sought not only to clear their loved ones' names but also to regain the rights and properties that had been stripped from them due to the convictions.

On October 17, 1711, the Massachusetts legislature passed an act that nullified the attainders of 22 people who had been convicted during the trials. This act was a significant step in reversing the legal wrongs committed during the witch hunt. However, it was by no means comprehensive or uniformly applied. While the act cleared the names of the 22 individuals, others, like Giles Corey, who had been pressed to death, were not included. Moreover, the legislative reversal did not bring with it automatic compensation for the families of the victims. It addressed the legal wrongs, but the emotional and financial toll that the trials had exacted on these families was left largely unaddressed.

The question of compensating the victims' families was particularly contentious. Many of the families had lost not only loved ones but also land, property, and livelihoods. For some, the reversal of the attainders was symbolic, but for others, it was a matter of financial survival. They wanted restitution for the years of hardship they had endured. The Massachusetts legislature approved £600 to be divided among the families who petitioned for compensation in 1711. However, this amount was far from adequate, and the way it was distributed led to further frustration.

The legal process of reversing attainders and compensating victims' families was an attempt at reconciliation, but it was incomplete at best. The financial compensation, while a gesture of goodwill, often failed to meet the real needs of the families who had been devastated by the trials. Many of these families had suffered not only the loss of loved ones but also the social stigma of being associated with convicted witches, a burden that no amount of money could erase.

The impact of these legal measures was mixed. For some, the act of reversing the attainders provided a sense of closure, a recognition that their loved ones had been wrongfully convicted. For others, especially those who had received little or no compensation, the process felt more like an empty gesture. The failure to fully address the material and emotional losses sustained by the families left many feeling that justice had not been fully served.

In the years that followed, the Salem witch trials became a dark chapter in Massachusetts' history, one that the colony would struggle to reckon with for generations. The efforts to reverse the attainders and compensate the victims' families were steps toward righting the wrongs of the past, but they could never fully undo the damage. The scars left by the trials were deep, and for many, the legal and financial reparations came too late to make a real difference.

The story of reversing the attainders and compensating the families is a reminder of the limits of legal justice in the face of profound human suffering. While the courts could clear a name and restore lost rights, they could not bring back the dead, heal the wounds of grief, or erase the stigma that the witch trials had cast over entire communities. However, the process of reconciliation was imperfect, much like the society that had allowed the trials to happen in the first place.

Salem's Transformation to Danvers

In the aftermath of the Salem witch trials of 1692, the transformation of Salem Village into Danvers stands as a powerful symbol of the community's desire to redefine itself. This change, more than a mere renaming, represented a deliberate attempt to distance itself from the agonizing aspect of its history and to forge a new identity.

The Motivation Behind the Name Change

The decision to rename Salem Village to Danvers in 1752 was motivated by a complex interplay of historical and social factors. The trials had left an indelible mark on the town's reputation, tainting its name with the specter of injustice and fanaticism. By the mid-18th century, there was a growing desire among the residents to escape the shadow of the past. Changing the name was a way to symbolically sever ties with the notorious events of 1692 and to signal a fresh start. The new name, Danvers, was chosen to honor Danvers Osborn, a prominent local figure, and to establish a distinct identity separate from the grim legacy of Salem.

Rebuilding Identity and Community Efforts

As Salem Village transitioned to Danvers, the community embarked on a concerted effort to rebuild and redefine itself. The early 18th century was a time of reconstruction and reformation. The townspeople focused on revitalizing their economy, which had been severely disrupted by the trials and subsequent social upheaval. Agriculture, which had once been the backbone of the village's economy, was reinvigorated with new techniques and improved practices. The town also saw a resurgence in trade and commerce, with the establishment of new businesses and the expansion of existing ones.

In addition to economic revitalization, there was a concerted effort to restore the town's social fabric. Public events, such as fairs and festivals, became a staple of community life, designed to foster unity and a sense of normalcy. The construction of new buildings and the renovation of old ones reflected the town's commitment to moving forward. Churches, schools, and meetinghouses were refurbished, not only to improve functionality but also to symbolize a new era of hope and prosperity.

Lasting Effects on Culture and Economy

The renaming and subsequent rebuilding efforts had significant and lasting effects on Danvers. Culturally, the town managed to create a new narrative that overshadowed the dark events of the past. The name Danvers became synonymous with resilience and renewal rather than fear and hysteria. This cultural shift was reflected in local traditions, with a focus on commemorating progress and community spirit rather than the trials.

Economically, Danvers benefited from the rebranding. The fresh start attracted new settlers and entrepreneurs, which stimulated growth and development. The town's economy diversified, with agriculture, trade, and manufacturing all contributing to its prosperity. The new identity as Danvers helped to attract investment and establish a reputation as a forward-looking, thriving community.

Contrasting Salem of 1692 with Danvers

To fully appreciate the transformation, one must contrast the Salem of 1692 with the Danvers that emerged in the mid-18th century. Salem in 1692 was a place plagued by paranoia and fear, where the witch trials had sown discord and division among neighbors. The community was deeply scarred, its social structures destabilized, and its reputation forever marred by the tragic events.

In contrast, Danvers in the 1750s and beyond was a community marked by recovery and progress. The town was bustling with new activity, its streets lined with well-maintained buildings and lively businesses. The people of Danvers were focused on building a positive future, their energy directed toward growth and renewal rather than the ghosts of the past.

This transformation from Salem to Danvers serves as a poignant reminder of the power of collective will and the capacity of communities to overcome their darkest moments. By renaming and rebuilding, Danvers not only erased the physical mark of its troubled past but also reimagined its place in history, ensuring that the story of its resilience would be the defining legacy of the town.

The Victims' Families: Generations of Guilt and Grief

The Salem Witch Trials of 1692 cast a long shadow over the families of both the accused and the accusers, creating a legacy of guilt, grief, and confusion that would span generations.

For the families of the victims, the trials left an indelible mark of sorrow and injustice. Take, for instance, the descendants of Rebecca Nurse, one of the most respected women in Salem Village who was convicted and executed despite her unwavering proclamations of innocence. Her great-great-grandson, Phineas Putnam, writing in the late 18th century, lamented, *"The stain upon our family name, though undeserved, has haunted us through the years. We carry the burden of knowing our ancestor died for naught but the fears and superstitions of men."*

This sentiment of inherited grief was common among the victims' families. Many struggled with a sense of powerlessness in the face of such a grave miscarriage of justice. Some, like the descendants of John Proctor, another executed victim, chose to leave Salem altogether, seeking to escape the painful memories and lingering stigma associated with their family name.

The Proctor family's exodus was not unusual. In the years following the trials, Salem saw a significant outflow of residents, many of whom were related to the accused. This diaspora spread the pain of Salem across New England and beyond, creating pockets of grief-stricken families trying to rebuild their lives away from the scene of their ancestors' torment.

On the other side of the coin, the families of the accusers grappled with a different kind of anguish – that of guilt and shame. The descendants of Ann Putnam Jr., one of the primary accusers, carried the weight of their ancestor's actions for centuries. In 1706, Ann publicly apologized for her role in the trials, but this act of contrition did little to alleviate the burden on future generations.

Sarah Putnam, a direct descendant of Ann, wrote in her diary in 1892, two hundred years after the trials: "The actions of my forebear hang heavy on my conscience, though I had no part in them. I often wonder how many innocent lives were destroyed by the words of a child, and how we can ever make amends for such a grievous wrong."

This sense of inherited guilt led many descendants of accusers to engage in acts of atonement. Some dedicated their lives to public service, others to the pursuit of justice and truth. The Putnam family, for instance, became known for their philanthropic efforts in Salem, quietly working to improve the community their ancestors had helped tear apart.

As the generations passed, the collective memory of Salem evolved. The initial shame and silence that shrouded the events gradually gave way to a desire for understanding and reconciliation. By the mid-19th century, there was a growing movement to acknowledge the injustices of the past and honor the memory of the victims.

This shift in perspective was exemplified by the efforts of John Proctor III, great-grandson of the executed John Proctor. In 1830, he successfully petitioned the Massachusetts legislature to reverse the attainder on his great-grandfather's name, officially clearing him of all charges. This act not only brought a measure of peace to the Proctor family but also marked a turning point in how Salem as a whole viewed its history.

The 20th century saw an even greater push for remembrance and reconciliation. In 1957, Ann Putnam's descendant, Charles Upham, played a crucial role in establishing the Salem Witch Trials Memorial. Speaking at the dedication ceremony, Upham said, "We cannot change the past, but we can acknowledge its errors and strive to learn from them. This memorial stands as a testament to our commitment to justice and our rejection of the fear and superstition that led to these tragic events."

Oral histories collected from descendants in the late 20th and early 21st centuries reveal the complex emotions still associated with the trials. Mary Eastey, a descendant of the accused Mary Eastey, shared in a 1998 interview: "Growing up, the trials were rarely discussed in our family. It was like a wound that never fully healed. But as I've grown older, I've come to see my ancestor's strength and dignity in the face of such injustice as a source of pride."

Similarly, Jonathan Corwin, a descendant of Judge Jonathan Corwin who presided over many of the trials, expressed a mix of regret and determination: "We can't change what our ancestors did, but we can work to ensure such injustices never happen again. It's a responsibility I feel deeply."

The legacy of the Salem Witch Trials continues to evolve. In recent years, there has been a renewed interest in genealogy and family history, leading many Americans to discover their connections to this dark chapter of colonial history. This has sparked new conversations about historical memory, justice, and the long-term impacts of persecution.

In 2022, Elizabeth Peterson, a descendant of both an accuser and an accused, organized a reconciliation ceremony in Salem. The event brought together descendants from both sides, fostering dialogue and understanding. "We're all carrying pieces of this history," Peterson remarked. "By coming together, we can start to heal wounds that have festered for generations."

The story of Salem's legacy is one of slow but steady progress towards acknowledgment and healing. From the initial silence and shame to the current efforts at reconciliation and education, the families affected by the trials have played a crucial role in shaping how we remember and interpret this chapter of American history.

As we look to the future, the descendants of Salem serve as a reminder of the enduring impact of historical injustices and the importance of confronting our past. Their stories of guilt, grief, resilience, and reconciliation offer valuable lessons about the long-term consequences of fear and persecution, as well as the power of acknowledgment and forgiveness in healing historical wounds.

The legacy of the Salem Witch Trials, as seen through the eyes of the victims' and accusers' families, is a testament to the complex ways in which history shapes our present and future. It reminds us that the past is never truly past, and that the actions of our ancestors can echo through generations, challenging us to confront difficult truths and strive for a more just and compassionate society.

CHAPTER 10

Legacy and Lessons

Salem in Popular Culture

The Salem witch trials of 1692, with their dark combination of fear, superstition, and injustice, have long held a grip on the imagination of popular culture. Literature, film, television, and other forms of media have explored these trials repeatedly, often blending historical fact with creative license to capture the audience's attention. In doing so, these portrayals have played a critical role in shaping the public's understanding of the events. As we survey these representations, we can see the power they have had in not only keeping the memory of Salem alive but also in distorting it at times to fit particular narratives, ideologies, and artistic visions.

Arthur Miller's The Crucible and Its Influence

No discussion of the Salem witch trials in popular culture can begin without acknowledging the profound influence of Arthur Miller's 1953 play The Crucible. Written during the height of McCarthyism in America, Miller used the Salem witch trials as an allegory for the Red Scare—a period of intense fear and paranoia about communism that led to widespread accusations, blacklisting, and the destruction of many careers. In The Crucible, Miller dramatizes the trials, capturing the mass hysteria and moral panic that engulfed Salem. Through the characters, particularly John Proctor and Abigail Williams, he exposes how fear, personal vendettas, and the collapse of rational thought lead to tragedy.

The play has had an enormous impact on how the Salem witch trials are remembered in the public consciousness. Miller's depiction of Salem as a town gripped by irrational fear and the corrupting influence of authority has led to a common association of the trials with themes of injustice and the dangers of authoritarianism. The Crucible has been adapted multiple times for film and television, perhaps most notably in the 1996 movie starring Daniel Day-Lewis and Winona Ryder. This adaptation brought Miller's play to a wider audience and further entrenched the view that the trials were primarily a result of mass hysteria.

However, while The Crucible has contributed to public awareness of the Salem witch trials, it also simplifies and fictionalizes many aspects of the historical events. For instance, the character of Abigail Williams, who serves as a key antagonist in the play, is portrayed as being much older than she actually was—she was 11 at the time of the trials, rather than the 17-year-old Miller depicts. Additionally, while the play suggests a romantic affair between John Proctor and Abigail, there is no historical evidence to support this. Such creative liberties, while serving Miller's dramatic and political goals, have shaped how audiences perceive the trials, often obscuring the more complex realities of what actually happened in 1692.

Film and Television: Horror and Drama

Beyond The Crucible, the Salem witch trials have been a popular subject in film and television, often as a backdrop for horror. Films like The Lords of Salem (2012), directed by Rob Zombie, take the trials and their legacy into the realm of supernatural horror. In this film, the descendants of the Salem witches seek revenge on the modern inhabitants of Salem, blending historical events with pure fantasy. While such movies have little to do with the historical reality of the trials, they reflect how Salem's past has become a fertile ground for exploring themes of witchcraft, the occult, and revenge from beyond the grave. The trials, in this context, become less about the historical events and more about serving as a symbol of paranoia and supernatural terror.

Television series like Salem (2014-2017) also take creative liberties with the history of the trials. In this show, the premise is that witches are real and are manipulating events in Salem to their advantage. The series takes viewers into a world where magic and witchcraft are tangible forces, feeding into modern audiences' fascination with the supernatural. While entertaining, such portrayals distance the public from the true nature of the Salem witch trials, where the real "witches" were innocent men and women caught in a web of superstition, religious extremism, and social tension.

On the more factual side, documentaries and historical dramas have also tackled the trials, often aiming to educate audiences about the real events. PBS's American Experience series produced an episode titled The Witch Trials of Salem that delves deeply into the historical context, presenting a more accurate and sobering picture of the trials. Such programs often serve as correctives to the fictionalized versions, providing historical evidence, expert interviews, and a detailed exploration of the social and religious dynamics that contributed to the panic.

Literature: From Historical Fiction to Fantasy

The Salem witch trials have also inspired countless works of literature, ranging from historical fiction to fantasy and even young adult novels. Works like The Heretic's Daughter by Kathleen Kent offer a more grounded, historically accurate account of the trials, told from the perspective of one of the accused women's daughters. Kent's novel, like many others in this genre, aims to humanize the victims of the trials, giving readers insight into the emotional and psychological toll of the events. Through fiction, authors like Kent provide a voice to the silenced, allowing readers to connect with the trials on a deeply personal level.

In contrast, other works take a more fantastical approach. Wicked Girls by Stephanie Hemphill is a young adult novel that reimagines the story of the "afflicted" girls who accused their neighbors of witchcraft, presenting them as complex characters caught up in a situation that spirals out of control. While still rooted in historical events, the novel uses creative license to explore the motivations and emotions behind the accusations, offering a more nuanced portrayal of the girls than simply seeing them as villains or victims.

The trials have even made their way into speculative fiction, such as in Deborah Harkness's A Discovery of Witches, where historical witch hunts serve as part of a broader mythology involving vampires, witches, and other supernatural beings. Such works demonstrate how deeply the image of Salem as a site of witchcraft has embedded itself in popular culture, allowing authors to blend history with fantasy to explore themes of power, persecution, and fear.

Shaping Public Perception

These varied portrayals, from Arthur Miller's politically charged drama to supernatural horror films and educational documentaries, have shaped how the public perceives the Salem witch trials. For many, the trials symbolize the dangers of hysteria, unchecked authority, and the consequences of scapegoating. In some cases, particularly in horror and fantasy, the trials become a canvas for exploring broader themes of witchcraft and the supernatural, often at the expense of historical accuracy.

The enduring fascination with Salem in popular culture speaks to the timeless nature of its themes—fear, power, and the consequences of mass delusion. While many of these portrayals take liberties with the facts, they ensure that the Salem witch trials remain a potent symbol in the public imagination, continuing to provoke thought and reflection on the darker sides of human nature.

Modern Interpretations and Scholarship

The Salem witch trials have long fascinated historians, social scientists, and the general public alike. Over the past century, numerous interpretations have emerged, each contributing to a more nuanced understanding of what transpired in 1692. Modern interpretations, particularly those from the 20th and 21st centuries, reflect the evolving methodologies and interdisciplinary approaches used by scholars to explore complex historical events. These interpretations have allowed historians to move beyond earlier explanations centered on religious fervor and mass hysteria, offering richer and more sophisticated analyses of the social, political, and psychological forces at play.

The Psychoanalytical Lens

In the early 20th century, one of the first modern interpretations of the Salem witch trials came through the psychoanalytical framework. Freud's theories, which had gained prominence at the time, provided a basis for exploring the inner psychological motivations behind the hysteria. Scholars like Marion Starkey, in her 1949 book The Devil in Massachusetts, applied these ideas to the trials. Starkey proposed that the girls who initiated the accusations suffered from repressed emotions and sexual anxieties, projecting their inner turmoil outward in the form of witchcraft accusations. This approach aligned with Freudian concepts of suppressed desires manifesting in destructive behavior, though it often sidelined broader social and cultural dynamics.

While psychoanalysis offered a compelling explanation for the behavior of the accusers, it fell short in explaining the systemic acceptance of these accusations by the wider community and the authorities. Starkey's work paved the way for further exploration into the psychological and emotional triggers of mass hysteria, but later scholars found this approach too narrow, demanding a more holistic view of the trials that included the political and religious dimensions.

The Social and Economic Context

By the mid-20th century, historians began to place greater emphasis on the social and economic factors that shaped the Salem witch trials. One of the most significant works of this period was Paul Boyer and Stephen Nissenbaum's Salem Possessed: The Social Origins of Witchcraft (1974). This groundbreaking study shifted the focus from individual psychological issues to the broader societal tensions brewing in Salem at the time. Boyer and Nissenbaum used quantitative methods—analyzing property records, tax lists, and village demographics—to show how economic disparities between Salem Village (where most of the accusers lived) and Salem Town (home to many of the accused) created a fertile ground for conflict.

Their thesis argued that the witch trials were in part a result of deep-seated social rivalries and economic grievances. Salem Village was largely agrarian and faced declining economic prospects, while Salem Town was becoming more commercially prosperous. This divide, they contended, fueled envy, resentment, and suspicion among the villagers, which in turn found expression through the witchcraft accusations. The accusers, many from struggling families, targeted wealthier members of

Salem Town, illustrating how economic inequalities and local power struggles intersected with religious fears.

Boyer and Nissenbaum's work was one of the first to employ a social history approach to the trials, examining how the everyday lives and economic conditions of the villagers shaped the accusations. Their methodology marked a shift away from viewing the trials as an isolated event of religious hysteria and toward understanding it as a reflection of deeper societal issues.

Feminist and Gender-Based Interpretations

Another significant scholarly shift in the interpretation of the Salem witch trials came with the rise of feminist history in the 1970s and 1980s. Scholars began to explore the gendered dimensions of the witch hunts, particularly the way women—who comprised the majority of the accused—were positioned within the patriarchal structures of Puritan society. Carol Karlsen's 1987 book The Devil in the Shape of a Woman is a landmark in this area of scholarship. Karlsen argued that the Salem trials reflected broader societal anxieties about women's roles and the ways in which women's economic independence and nonconformity threatened the established social order.

Karlsen noted that many of the accused women were either widows with property or women who had inherited wealth, which made them targets in a society where women's power was typically circumscribed. The trials, in this view, were a means of controlling or punishing women who defied conventional gender roles, whether by asserting financial independence or simply by not conforming to societal expectations of female behavior. This gendered interpretation opened up new avenues of understanding not only the Salem trials but also the broader phenomenon of witch hunts in early modern Europe.

Feminist interpretations of Salem reframed the trials as a form of social control, where accusations of witchcraft were used to maintain patriarchal norms. This perspective remains influential in contemporary scholarship, as historians continue to explore how gender, power, and societal expectations intersected in 17th-century New England.

The Role of Religion and Puritanism

Religion, particularly the strict Puritan belief system that dominated Salem at the time, remains a critical factor in understanding the trials. However, modern scholars have moved beyond simplistic explanations of "religious fanaticism" to explore the deeper theological and spiritual anxieties that shaped the witch hunts. Historian David D. Hall's work in the late 20th century focused on how Puritan theology, particularly its emphasis on the invisible world of spirits and the devil's ability to corrupt even the most pious souls, created an environment where witchcraft accusations were not only possible but almost inevitable.

Hall's scholarship examines how Puritan clergy played a dual role in both fueling and moderating the witchcraft panic. While some ministers supported the trials, others expressed skepticism and sought to limit the use of spectral evidence—testimony based on visions and dreams—which was crucial to many of the accusations. This debate within the Puritan leadership itself shows how religion, far from being a monolithic force, was a site of contestation during the trials.

Interdisciplinary Approaches and New Methods

The most recent scholarship on Salem has been characterized by interdisciplinary approaches that draw on methods from anthropology, psychology, sociology, and even environmental science. One notable example is

Mary Beth Norton's In the Devil's Snare (2002), which links the witch trials to the broader geopolitical context of King William's War, a conflict between English settlers and Native Americans on the New England frontier. Norton suggests that the ongoing war, which brought violence, displacement, and uncertainty to the region, created an atmosphere of fear and paranoia that contributed to the witchcraft accusations. This analysis places the Salem trials within a larger context of colonial conflict and insecurity, moving beyond purely local or psychological explanations.

In recent years, scholars have also employed digital history techniques to reanalyze the court records, providing new insights into the social networks and patterns of accusation. This use of data-driven methods allows historians to track relationships between accusers and accused in unprecedented detail, offering fresh perspectives on how the trials unfolded.

Modern interpretations of the Salem witch trials have moved far beyond the early psychological or religious explanations, incorporating social, economic, gender-based, and geopolitical perspectives. The use of interdisciplinary methods has deepened our understanding of the trials, revealing them to be a complex event shaped by multiple forces.

Echoes of Salem: Mass Hysteria in the Modern World

The Salem witch trials of 1692 are often viewed through the lens of history as a unique and bizarre episode, a relic of a bygone era where superstition held sway over rational thought. However, when examined more closely, the patterns of fear, suspicion, and mass hysteria that characterized Salem are not as foreign to the modern world as one might hope. In fact, parallels can be drawn between Salem and numerous instances of mass hysteria or moral panics in more recent history. These events, despite their different contexts and timelines, share common psychological and social factors that can help us understand why such phenomena continue to occur—and more importantly, what can be done to prevent them.

Psychological Factors: Fear, Uncertainty, and the Human Mind

One of the most significant psychological factors behind both the Salem witch trials and modern cases of mass hysteria is fear, particularly fear of the unknown or of forces perceived to be beyond one's control. In Salem, the Puritans lived in a world teeming with religious dogma and uncertainty. Disease, Native American raids, and harsh living conditions were common, and the threat of spiritual and physical dangers weighed heavily on their minds. These factors created an environment ripe for scapegoating and a collective descent into paranoia.

A comparable situation occurred during the Red Scare of the 1950s, when the fear of communism permeated American society. Much like the Salem villagers, Americans were faced with an invisible threat—this time, not witches, but communist infiltrators supposedly hiding within the nation's borders, waiting to undermine democratic institutions. The infamous actions of Senator Joseph McCarthy and the House Un-American Activities Committee (HUAC) fueled this paranoia, leading to the persecution of many innocent people who were accused of communist sympathies. Just as in Salem, mere suspicion was enough to destroy lives and careers.

In both cases, the fear of unseen, malevolent forces was stoked by authority figures and amplified by the social dynamics of small, close-knit communities. This leads us to another critical psychological element: the power of suggestion and groupthink. In times of crisis, people tend to look to authority figures for guidance. In Salem, figures like Reverend Samuel Parris fanned the flames of witch hysteria by validating the claims of young girls who accused their neighbors of witchcraft. Similarly, during the Red Scare, McCarthy's accusations went largely unchallenged, as the political and social climate made it dangerous for individuals to question the legitimacy of his claims.

Social Dynamics: Us vs. Them

At the heart of both the Salem witch trials and modern cases of mass hysteria is the creation of an "us vs. them" mentality. In Salem, those accused of witchcraft were often outsiders in some way—they were women, widows, or individuals who didn't conform to the strict social and religious norms of Puritan society. Their differences made them easy targets, and their supposed guilt served as a way for the community to externalize their fears and project them onto a select group of scapegoats.

This same dynamic played out during the AIDS crisis of the 1980s. As the disease began to spread, many Americans—fueled by misinformation and fear—began to view homosexual men and drug users as the primary culprits. Homophobia and moral judgments clouded the public's ability to respond to the crisis rationally, much like the religious fervor and superstition in Salem hindered a fair and reasoned investigation of the witchcraft accusations. The social and cultural *"othering"* of certain groups made it easier for the larger population to point fingers and place blame, rather than address the root causes of their fear.

Another modern parallel can be found in the Satanic Panic of the 1980s and early 1990s. Fueled by sensationalist media reports, the public became convinced that underground Satanic cults were abusing children across the United States. Much like Salem, the Satanic Panic was driven by allegations that were often based on flimsy or outright fabricated evidence. The accusers, many of whom were children themselves, mirrored the role of the young girls in Salem whose testimonies launched the witch trials. In both cases, the authorities' acceptance of these unsubstantiated claims allowed the hysteria to spread unchecked.

Media's Role in Amplifying Agitation

One major difference between the Salem witch trials and modern instances of mass hysteria is the role of the media in amplifying fear and spreading misinformation. While Salem's news traveled slowly by word of mouth or written letters, today's world is dominated by instant communication, and the 24-hour news cycle has the power to stoke fear and moral panic with unprecedented speed.

Consider the Y2K scare at the turn of the millennium. In the late 1990s, fear spread that computer systems around the world would malfunction when the calendar turned to the year 2000, potentially leading to massive infrastructure failures. Though the issue was based on legitimate concerns within the tech world, the media's sensationalist coverage amplified the potential consequences, leading to widespread panic that was ultimately unwarranted.

In a similar vein, the COVID-19 pandemic provided fertile ground for mass hysteria, as misinformation and conspiracy theories spread rapidly across social media platforms. While many people reacted rationally to the pandemic, there was also a rise in bizarre beliefs, from the idea that 5G networks were spreading the virus to the baseless claim that the virus was a hoax. This echoes Salem's climate of fear and the spread of falsehoods that contributed to the persecution of supposed witches.

Lessons from Salem: Understanding and Preventing Future Panics

What can we learn from Salem, and how can these lessons help us prevent future instances of mass hysteria and moral panic? One critical lesson is the importance of skepticism and the need to question authority and popular opinion in times of crisis. In Salem, very few individuals were willing to challenge the legitimacy of the witch trials, and those who did—such as Giles Corey and Rebecca Nurse—paid with their lives. A similar phenomenon occurred during the Red Scare, when those who opposed McCarthy's methods were labeled communist sympathizers themselves.

To prevent such events in the future, it is essential to foster an environment where people feel safe questioning dominant narratives, particularly when those narratives involve the scapegoating of marginalized or vulnerable groups. This involves a strong commitment to education, critical thinking, and the promotion of media literacy, especially in today's world, where information—and misinformation—spreads so quickly.

Additionally, understanding the psychological and social dynamics that fuel mass rampage is crucial. Fear and uncertainty are powerful motivators, but they can be counteracted with clear communication, transparent leadership, and policies that address people's underlying anxieties rather than feeding them. The Salem witch trials serve as a stark reminder of what can happen when fear is allowed to spiral out of control, and the many echoes of Salem in modern history show that we must remain vigilant to ensure that such tragedies do not repeat themselves.

Conclusion

Thank you for joining me on this journey through one of the most fascinating and troubling chapters of American history. I hope that by exploring the Salem witch trials together, we've not only gained a deeper understanding of this pivotal event, but also discovered its relevance to our modern world.

Writing this book has been a labor of love, driven by a passion to shed light on the complex human stories behind the infamous trials. It's my sincere hope that these pages have brought the people of Salem to life for you - their fears, their struggles, and their humanity.

If you've found value in this exploration of the Salem witch hunt, I would be incredibly grateful if you could take a moment to share your thoughts on Amazon. Your honest review and rating can help other readers discover this book and continue the important conversation about the lessons we can learn from history.

Thank you again for your time and for being part of this historical journey. Your support means the world to me and to all those who work to keep history alive and relevant. Together, we can ensure that the lessons of Salem continue to inform and inspire future generations.

Printed in Great Britain
by Amazon